Howard Pyle

The Rose of Paradise

Howard Pyle

The Rose of Paradise

ISBN/EAN: 9783744689328

Printed in Europe, USA, Canada, Australia, Japan

Cover: Foto ©Thomas Meinert / pixelio.de

More available books at **www.hansebooks.com**

"BOAT AHOY!" I CRIED OUT, AND THEN LEVELLED MY PISTOL AND FIRED.

THE ROSE OF PARADISE

*Being a detailed account of certain adventures that
happened to Captain John Mackra, in connection
with the famous pirate, Edward England, in
the year 1720, off the Island of Juanna
in the Mozambique Channel; writ
by himself, and now for the
first time published*

By HOWARD PYLE

AUTHOR OF

" PEPPER AND SALT " " THE WONDER CLOCK " ETC.

ILLUSTRATED

NEW YORK

HARPER & BROTHERS, FRANKLIN SQUARE

1888

ILLUSTRATIONS.

THE ROSE OF PARADISE.

I.

ALTHOUGH the account of the serious engagement betwixt the *Cassandra* and the two pirate vessels in the Mozambique Channel hath already been set to print, the publick have yet to know many lesser and more detailed circumstances concerning the matter;* and as the above-mentioned account hath caused much remark and comment, I

---

* A brief narration of the naval engagement between Captain Mackra and the two pirate vessels was given in the Captain's official report made at Bombay. It appears in the life of the pirate England in Johnson's book: "A Genuine Account of the Voyages and Plunders of the Most Notorious Pyrates, &c." London, 1742.

I

shall take it upon me to give many inci-
dents not yet known, seeking to render
them neither in refined rhetorick nor with
romantick circumstances such as are sometimes used by novel and story writers to
catch the popular attention, but telling this
history as directly, and with as little verbos-
ity and circumlocution, as possible.

For the conveniency of the reader, I shall
render this true and veracious account under sundry headings, marked I., II., III., &c.,
as seen above, which may assist him in sep-
arating the less from the more notable por-
tions of the narrative.

According to my log—a diary or journal
of circumstances appertaining to shipboard
—it was the nineteenth day of April, 1720,
when, I being in command of the East India
Company's ship *Cassandra*, billed for Bombay and waiting for orders to sail, comes
Mr. Evans, the Company's agent, aboard with
certain sealed and important orders which

he desired to deliver to me at the last minute.

After we had come to my cabin and were
set down, Mr. Evans hands me two pacquets,
one addressed to myself, the other superscribed to one Benjamin Longways.

He then proceeded to inform me that the
Company had a matter of exceeding import
and delicacy which they had no mind to intrust to any one but such, he was pleased to
say, as was a tried and worthy servant, and
that they had fixed upon me as the fitting
one to undertake the commission, which was
of such a nature as would involve the transfer of many thousand pounds. He furthermore informed me that a year or two before,
the Company had rendered certain aid to
the native King of Juanna, an island lying
between Madagascar and the east coast of
Africa, at a time when there was war betwixt him and the king of an island called
Mohilla, which lyeth coadjacent to the other
country; that I should make Juanna upon

my voyage, and that I should there receive through Mr. Longways, who was the Company's agent at that place, a pacquet of the greatest import, relating to the settlement of certain matters betwixt the East India Company and the king of that island. Concluding his discourse, he further said that he had no hesitation in telling me that the pacquet which I would there receive from Mr. Longways concerned certain payments due the East India Company, and would, as he had said before, involve the transfer of many thousand pounds; from which I might see what need there was of great caution and circumspection in the transaction.

" But, sir," says I, "sure the Company is making a prodigious mistake in confiding a business of such vast importance as this to one so young and so inexperienced as I."

To this Mr. Evans only laughed, and was pleased to say that it was no concern of his, but from what he had observed he thought the honorable Company had made a good choice, and that of a keen tool, in my case. He furthermore said that in the pacquet which he had given to me, and which was addressed to me, I would find such detailed instructions as would be necessary, and that the other should be handed to Mr. Longways, and was an order for the transfer above spoken of.

Soon after this he left the ship, and was rowed ashore, after many kind and complacent wishes for a quick and prosperous voyage.

It may be as well to observe here as elsewhere within this narrative that the Company's written orders to me contained little that Mr. Evans had not told me, saving only certain details, and the further order that that which the agent at Juanna should transfer to me should be delivered to the Governor at Bombay, and that I should receive a written receipt from him for the same. Neither at that time did I know the nature of the trust that I was called upon to execute, save that it was of great import, and that it involved money to some mightily considerable amount.

The crew of the *Cassandra* consisted of fifty-one souls all told, officers and ordinary seamen. Besides these were six passengers, the list of whom I give below, it having been copied from my log-book journal :

Captain Edward Leach (of the East India Company's service).

Mr. Thomas Fellows (who was to take the newly established agency of the Company at Cuttapore).

Mr. John Williamson (a young cadet).

Mrs. Colonel Evans (a sister-in-law of the Company's agent spoken of above).

Mistress Pamela Boon (a niece of the Governor at Bombay).

Mistress Ann Hastings (the young lady's waiting-woman).

Of Mistress Pamela Boon I feel extreme delicacy in speaking, not caring to make publick matters of such a nature as our subse-

quent relations to one another. Yet this
much I may say without indelicacy, that she
was at that time a young lady of eighteen
years of age, and that her father, who had
been a clergyman, having died the year before, she was at that time upon her way to
India to join her uncle, who, as said above,
was Governor at Bombay, and had been left
her guardian.

Nor will it be necessary to tire the reader
by any disquisition upon the other passengers, excepting Captain Leach, whom I shall
have good cause to remember to the very
last day of my life.

He was a tall, handsome fellow, of about
eight-and-twenty years of age, of good natural parts, and of an old and honorable family
of Hertfordshire. He was always exceedingly kind and pleasant to me, and treated
me upon every occasion with the utmost
complacency, and yet I conceived a most
excessive dislike for his person from the
very first time that I beheld him, nor, as

events afterwards proved, were my instincts astray, or did they mislead me in my sentiments, as they are so apt to do upon similar occasions.

After a voyage somewhat longer than usual, and having stopped at St. Helena, which hath of late been one of our stations, we sighted the southern coast of Madagascar about the middle of July, and on the eighteenth dropped anchor in a little bay on the eastern side of the island of Juanna, not being able to enter into the harbor which lyeth before the king's town because of the shallowness of the water and the lack of a safe anchorage, which is mightily necessary along such a treacherous and dangerous coast. In the same harbor we found two other vessels—one the *Greenwich*, Captain Kirby, an English ship; the other an Ostender, a great, clumsy, tub-shaped craft.

I was much put about that I could get no nearer to the king's town than I then was, it being some seven or eight leagues away around the northern end of the island. I was the more vexed that we could not well come to it in boats, other than by a long reach around the cape to the northward, which would increase the journey to wellnigh thirty miles. Besides all this, I was further troubled upon learning from Captain Kirby of the *Greenwich* that the pirates had been very troublesome in these waters for some time past. He said that having been ashore soon after he had come to that place, in search of a convenient spot to take in water, he had found fourteen pirates that had come in their canoes from the Mayotta, where the pirate ship to which they belonged, viz., the *Indian Queen*, two hundred and fifty tons, twenty-eight guns, and ninety men, commanded by Captain Oliver de la Bouche, bound from the Guinea coast to the East Indies, had been bulged and lost.

I asked Captain Kirby what he had done with the rogues. He told me, nothing at all, and that the less one had to do with such fellows the better. At this I was vastly surprised, and that he had taken no steps to put an end to such a nest of vile, wicked, and bloody-minded wretches when he had it so clearly in his power to take fourteen of them at once; more especially as he should have known that if they got away from that place and to any of their companions they would bring the others not only about his ears, but of every other craft that might be lying in the harbor at the time. Something to this effect I said, whereat he flew into a mighty huff, and said that if I had seen half the experience that he had been through I would not be so free in my threats of doing this or that to a set of wretches no better than so many devils from hell, who would cut a man's throat without any scruples either of fear or remorse.

To all this I made no rejoinder, for the pirates were far enough away by this time, and I was willing to suppose that Captain Kirby had done what he judged to be best in the matter. Yet the getting away of those evil wretches brought more trouble upon me than had happened in all my life before.

But, as was said before, I was in a pretty tub of pickle with all those things; for I could not bring my ship to anchor in any reasonable distance of the king's town, nor could I leave her and go on such a journey as would take a day or more, lest the pirates should come along in my absence. Neither did I like to send any of the officers under me to execute the commission, it being one of such exceeding delicacy and secrecy. At this juncture, and all of my passengers knowing that we could not leave that place till I had communicated certain papers to the Company's agent at the king's town, comes Captain Leach to me and volunteers to deliver the pacquet addressed to Mr. Longways. At first I was but little inclined to accept of his complacency, but having a secret feeling that I might be wronging him by my prejudice against him, I determined to give second thought to the matter before I hastily declined his offer of aid. Indeed, I may truthfully say I would have felt more inclined to refuse his assistance if I had entertained a more high opinion of his person. As it was, I could see no reason for not accepting his offer; he was regarded everywhere as a man of rectitude and of honor, and I had no real grounds to impeach this opinion; so the end of the business was that I accepted his aid with the best face that I was able to command, though that was with no very good grace, and gave him leave to choose ten volunteers as a boat's crew for the expedition.

II.

(THE reader will be pleased to observe
that, in pursuance of the plan above indi-
cated, I here begin a second part or chap-
ter of my narrative, the first dealing with
our voyage out as far as the island of Juanna, and matters of a kindred nature, whilst
the following relates to an entirely different
subject, namely, the nature of the trust imposed upon me, mention only of which has
heretofore been made.)

I do not now nor ever have believed that
Captain Leach had any other designs in of-
fering to execute my commission than that
of seizing so excellent an opportunity to see
a strange country and people after a long
and tiresome voyage upon the sea. Nevertheless, my allowing him to go was one of
the greatest mistakes in all of my whole life,

and cost me dearly enough before I had redeemed it.

The expedition under him was gone for three days, at the end of which time he returned, in company with a great canoe manned by a crew of about twenty tall, strapping black fellows, and with two or three sitting in the stern-sheets of the craft, bedecked with feathers and beads, whom I knew to be chiefs or warriors.

In the *Cassandra's* boat was a stranger who sat beside Captain Leach, talking very gayly, and who I knew could be none other than Mr. Longways, the Company's agent.

So soon as the *Cassandra's* boat had come alongside he skipped up the side like a monkey, and gave me a very civil bow immediately his feet touched the deck, which I returned with all the gravity I was able to command.

Mr. Longways was a lean, slim little man, and was dressed with great care, and in the very latest fashion that he could obtain;

from which, and his polite, affected manners and grimaces, I perceived that he rarely had the opportunity of coming upon board of a craft where there were ladies as passengers.

After Mr. Longways came Captain Leach, and after him the three great, tall, native chiefs, half naked, and with hair dressed after a most strange, curious fashion. At first they would have prostrated themselves at my feet, but I prevented them; whereupon they took my hand and set it upon their heads, which was anything but pleasant, their hair being thick with gums and greases.

I presently led the way to my cabin, the chiefs following close at our heels, and Mr. Longways walking beside me, grimacing like a little old monkey in a vastly affected manner. Nor could I forbear smiling to see how he directed his observations towards the ladies, and more especially Mistress Pamela, who stood at the rail of the deck above.

Mr. Longways carried in his hand a strong iron despatch-box, about the bigness of those used by the runners at the Bank, and so soon as we had come into my cabin he clapped it down upon the table with a great noise.

"There!" says he, fetching a deep sigh; "I, for one, am glad to be quit of it."

"Why," says I, "Mr. Longways, is there then so much in the little compass of that box?"

"Indeed yes," says he; "enough to make you and me rich men for our lives."

"I wonder, then," says I, laughing, "that you should bring it so easily to me, when you might have made off with it yourself, and no one the wiser."

"No, no," says he, quite seriously, without taking my jest, and jerking his head towards the black chiefs, who had squatted down upon their hams nigh to the table—"No, no. Our friends yonder have had their eyes on me sharply enough, though they do not understand one single word that we are saying to one another."

While we had been conversing I had fetched out a decanter of port and five glasses, and had poured out wine for all hands, which the black men drank with as great pleasure as Mr. Longways and myself.

After Mr. Longways had finished, he smacked his lips and set down his glass with a great air. "And now," says he, with a comical grimace of vanity and self-importance, "let us to business without loss of more time. First of all, I have to ask you, sir, do you know what all this treasure is for?"

I told him yes; that Mr. Evans had informed me that it was as payment for certain aid which the East India Company had rendered to the king of that country.

"And how," says he, very slowly, and cocking his head upon one side—"and how do you think our King Coffee is to make such payments? By bills upon the Bank

2

of Africa? No, no. The treasure is all in this box, every farthing of it; and I, sir, have been chosen by the honorable East India Company to have sole and entire charge of it for more than two weeks past." Here he looked at me very hard, as though he thought I would have made some remark upon what he had told me; but as I said nothing he presently resumed his discourse, after his own fashion. " I see," says he, "that you do not appreciate the magnitude of the trust that hath been imposed upon me. I shall show you, sir." And without more ado he fetched up a bunch of keys out of his pocket. He looked at them one after another until he found one some-what smaller than the rest, and with very curiously wrought guards. " Look at this," says he; "there are only three in the world like it. I hold one, King Coffee the other, and the Governor of Bombay the third." So saying, he thrust the key into the lock of the despatch-box.

"Stop a bit, sir," said I, very seriously, and laying my hand on his arm. "Have you very well considered what you are doing? Mr. Evans, the Company's agent, said nothing to me concerning the nature of the trust that was to be imposed upon me further than it was of very great value; and without you have received instructions to tell me further concerning this business, I much misdoubt that the Company intended me to be further informed as to its nature."

"Why, look'ee, Captain Mackra," says he, testily, "Tom Evans is one man and I am another, and I tell you further that I am as important an agent as he, even though he does live in London and I in this outrageous heathen country. Even if I had not intended showing you this treasure before, I would show it to you now, for I do not choose that anybody should think that Tom Evans is a man of more importance than I." So saying, and without more ado, he gave a quick turn to the key, and flung back the lid of the box.

I happened just then to glance at the three chiefs, and saw that they were watching us as a cat watches at a mouse-hole; but so soon as they saw me observing them they turned their eyes away so quickly that I hardly felt sure that I had seen them.

Inside of the box was a great lot of dried palm-leaf fibre wrapped around a ball of cotton, which Mr. Longways lifted very carefully and gently. Opening this, he came upon a little roll of dressed skin like the chamois-leather such as the jewellers and watch-makers use, and which was tied all about very carefully with a stout cord of palm fibre. Mr. Longways began laboriously to untie the knot in this cord, and, though I cannot tell why, there was something about the whole business that set my heart to beating very thickly and heavily within my breast.

Mr. Longways looked up under his brows at me with a very curious leer. " Did you ever hear," says he, " of The Rose of Paradise ?"

MR. LONGWAYS LOOKED UP UNDER HIS BROWN EYES AT ME WITH A VERY CURIOUS LEER.

I shook my head.

"Then I'll show her to you," said he; and he began unwinding the cord from about the roll of soft leather, the folds of which he presently opened. Then, as I looked down into his hand and saw what lay within the dressed skin, I was so struck with amazement that I could not find either breath or tongue to utter one single word.

III.

It was a ruby, the most beautiful I had ever seen, and about the bigness of a pigeon's egg.

At the sight of this prodigious jewel I was so disturbed in my spirits that I trembled as though with an ague, while the sweat started out of my forehead in great drops. "For the love of the Lord, put it up, man!" I cried, so soon as I could find breath and wits.

There was something in my voice that must have frightened Mr. Longways, for he looked mightily disturbed and taken aback; but he presently tried to pass it off for a jest. "Come, come," says he, as he wrapped up the stone in the soft leather again— "come, come; it's all between friend and friend, and no harm done."

But to this I answered not a word, but
began walking up and down the cabin, so
affected by what I had seen that I could
neither recover my spirits nor regain my
composure. The more I thought over the
business the less I liked it; for if anything
should now happen to the stone, and it
should be lost, every suspicion would fall
upon me, since I was possessed of the
knowledge of the value of that which was
given into my charge. I could not but
marvel at the foolish and magpie vanity of
Mr. Longways that should thus lead him to
betray to an unknown stranger what even
I, though so ignorant of the value of such
gems, could easily perceive was a vast in-
calculable treasure such as would make
any one man rich for a whole lifetime; and
even to this very day it is a matter of ad-
miration to me why the East India Company should have put such a man in a
place of important trust, the only reason
that I can assign being that no better man

could be found to take the agency in that place.

" Look'ee," said I, turning to him sudden-ly, " have you told of this jewel, this Rose of Paradise, to any one else ?"

" Why—" says he ; and then he stopped, and began gnawing his nether lip in a pee-vish fashion.

" Come, come," says I, "speak out plain, Master Longways, for this is no time for dilly-dallying."

" Well," says he, blurting out his words, " I did say something of it to Captain Leach, who, I would have you know, is a gentleman, and a man of honor into the bargain."

"And tell me," said I, paying no atten-tion to his braggadocio air, " did you show the stone to him also ?"

He looked up and down, as though not knowing what to say.

" Come, come, sir," said I, sternly, after waiting for a moment or two and he not answering me — "come, come, sir, I should like to have an answer, if you please. You will recollect that this trust now concerns not only you, but also myself, and if anything happens to the jewel I will be called upon to answer for it as well as yourself; so, as I said, you will answer my question."

"Why," says he, " Master Captain, and what if I did? Do you mean to impeach the honor of Captain Leach? I did show it to him one day when we stopped along the beach for water, if you must be told; but I can promise you that not another soul but yourself has seen it since I gave King Coffee my written receipt for it."

I made no more comment, but began again to walk up and down the cabin, vastly disturbed in my mind by all that I heard. Nothing could be gained by blaming the poor fool, who all this time sat watching me with a mightily troubled and disquieted face. "Sir," said I, at last, turning to him— "sir, I do not believe that you know what a

serious piece of folly you have committed
in this business.   By rights I should have
nothing more to do with the matter, but
should leave you to settle it with the Company as you choose ; but my instructions
were to deliver the stone at Bombay, and I
will undertake to do my part to the best of
my power.   I have nothing of blame to say
to you, but I must tell you plain that I cannot have you longer about my ship ; I do
not wish to order you to leave, but I will be
vastly obliged to you if you can return to
the king's town without longer stay."

At this address Mr. Longways grew very
red in the face.   " Sir ! sir !" he cried, " do
you dare to order me, an agent of the East
India Company, to leave one of that Company's own ships ?"

" That," said I, " you must salt to suit
your own taste."

" Very well !" cried he ; " give me a receipt for the stone and I'll go, though I tell
you plain that the Company shall hear of

the fashion in which you have been pleased to treat me."

I made no further answer to his words, but sat down and wrote out the receipt, specifying, however, the manner in which The Rose of Paradise had been shown both to Captain Leach and to myself.

For a while Mr. Longways hotly refused to accept it in the form in which it was writ; but finding that he could get no better, and that he would either have to accept of it or retain the stone in his own keeping until some further opportunity offered for consigning it to Bombay, he was finally fain to take what he could get, whereupon he folded up the paper and thrust it into his pocket, and then left the cabin with a vast show of dignity, and without so much as looking at me or saying a word to me.

He and the chiefs got into the great canoe, and rowed away whence they had come, and I saw no more of him until above a week afterwards, of which I shall have more to say further on in my narration.

IV.

I DID not go upon deck immediately after Mr. Longways had left the cabin, but sat there concerned with a great multitude of thoughts, and gazing absently at the box that held the treasure, and at the empty glasses with the dregs of the wine in the bottom.

Just in front of me was a small looking-glass fastened against the port side of the cabin in such position that by merely raising my eyes I could see the cabin door from where I sat.

In the upper part of the door was a little window of two panes of glass, which opened out under the overhang of the poop-deck.

Though I do not know what it was, something led me to glance up from where I sat, and in the glass I saw Captain Leach looking in at that window with a mightily strange expression on his face. He was not looking at me, but at the iron despatch-box upon the table, and I sat gazing at him for about the space of eight or ten seconds, in which time he moved neither his glance nor his person. Suddenly he lifted his eyes and looked directly into the glass, and his gaze met mine. I had thought that he would have been struck with confusion, and for a moment it did seem as though his look faltered, but he instantly recovered himself, and tapped lightly upon the door, and I bade him come in without moving where I sat.

He did as he was told, and sat down upon the chair which Mr. Longways had occupied only a few moments before. I confess that I was both frightened and angry at finding him thus, as it were, spying upon me, so that it was a moment or two before I trusted myself to speak.

"Sir," said I at last, "sure this voyage hath been long enough for you to know that the courtesies of shipboard require you to send a message to the captain to find whether he be disengaged or no."

Captain Leach showed no emotion at my reproof. "Captain Mackra," said he, quietly, "I do not know what that gabbling fool of an agent has or has not said to you, but I tell you plain he hath chosen to betray to me certain important matters concerning the East India Company, and that in yonder despatch-box is a large ruby, valued at nigh three hundred and fifty thousand pounds sterling."

I may confess that I was vastly amazed at the value of the stone, which was far greater than I had conceived a notion of, but I strove to show nothing of my sentiments to my interlocutor.

"Well, sir?" said I, looking him straight in the face.

He seemed somewhat struck aback at my manner, but he presently laughed lightly. "You take the matter with most admirablè coolness," said he; "far more than I would do were I in your place. But at least you will now perceive why I chose rather to come to you of myself than to send a messenger to you where a matter of such delicacy was concerned."

" Well, sir?" said I.

Captain Leach looked for a moment or two as though at a loss what next to say, but he presently spoke again. " I came to you," said he, " not knowing, as I said before, whether or no Mr. Longways had be- . trayed to you, as he has to me, the value of the trust imposed upon you ; and as I myself am now unfortunately concerned in the knowledge of this treasure, and so share in your responsibility, I come hither to discover what steps you propose taking to insure the safety of the stone."

Now it hath come under my observation that if a man be permitted to talk without let or stay, he will sooner or later betray that which lieth upon his mind. So from the very moment that Captain Leach uttered his last speech I conceived the darkest and most sinister suspicions of his purposes; nor from that time did I trust one single word that he said, or repose confidence in any of his actions, but was ready to see in everything something to awaken my doubts of his rectitude. Nor did these sentiments arise entirely from his words, but equally as much from my having discovered him, as it were, so prying upon my privacy.

"Sir," said I, rising from my seat, "I am infinitely obliged to you for your kindness in this affair, but as I have at present matters of considerable import that demand my closest attention, I must beg you to excuse me."

Captain Leach looked at me for a moment or two as though he had it upon his mind to say something further. However, he did not speak, but rising, delivered a very profound bow, and left the cabin without another word.

But there was no gainsaying the wisdom of the advice which he had given me as to concealing the treasure. Accordingly I obtained from the carpenter a basket of tools, and, bearing in mind the late visit with which he had favored me, having shaded the little window in the door of my cabin, I stripped off my coat and waistcoat, and after an hour or so of work, made shift to rig up a very snug little closet with a hinged door, in the bottom of my berth and below the mattress, wherein I hid the jewel. After that I breathed more freely, for I felt that the treasure could not be discovered without a long and careful search, the opportunities for which were not likely to occur.

Although my interview with Captain Leach might seem of small and inconsiderable moment to any one coolly reading this narrative in the privacy of his closet, yet coming to me as it did upon the heels of my other interview with Mr. Longways, it cast me into such disquietude of spirit as

3

I had not felt for a long time. I would have heaved anchor and away, without losing one single minute of delay, had it been possible for me to have done so; but not a breath of air was stirring, and there was nothing for it but to ride at anchor where we were, though, what with the heat and delay, it was all that I could do not to chafe myself into a fume of impatience.

So passed the day until about four o'clock in the afternoon, when there happened a certain thing that, had thunder and lightning burst from a clear sky, it could not have amazed me more. I being in my cabin at the time, comes Mr. Langely, my first mate, with the strange news that the lookout had sighted a vessel over the point of land to the southward. I could hardly accredit what he said, for, as above stated, not a breath of air was going. I hurried out of my cabin and upon deck, where I found Mr. White, the second mate, standing at the port side of the ship, with a glass in his hand directed a few points west of south, and over a spit of land which ran out in the channel towards that quarter, at which place the cape was covered by a mightily thick growth of scrub-bushes, with here and there a tall palm-tree rising from the midst of the thickets. Over beyond these I could see the thin white masts of the vessel that the lookout had sighted. There was no need of the glass, for I could see her plain enough, though not of what nature she might be. However, I took the telescope from Mr. White's hands, and made a long and careful survey of the stranger, but as much to hide my thoughts as for any satisfaction that I could gain; for what confounded me beyond measure was that a vessel should be sighted so suddenly, and in a dead calm, where I felt well assured no craft had been for days past. Nor was I less amazed to find, as I held the stranger steadfastly in the circle of the object-glass, a tall palm-tree being almost betwixt the

Cassandra and her, and almost directly in
my line of sight, that she was slowly and
steadily making way towards the northward,
and at a very considerable angle with the
Gulf current, which there had a set more to
the westward than where we lay at anchor.

I think that all, or nearly all, of my passengers were upon the poop-deck at that
time, Captain Leach with a pocket field-
glass which he had fetched with him from
England, and with which he was directing
Mistress Pamela's observation to the strange
craft.   Nearly all the crew were also watching her by this time, and in a little while
they perceived, what I had seen from the
first, that the vessel was by some contrivance making head without a breath of wind,
and nearly against the Gulf current.

As for the stranger herself, so far as I
could judge, seeing nothing of her hull, she
was a bark of somewhat less tonnage than
the *Cassandra;* and the masts, which we
could perceive very clearly against the clear

sky, had a greater rake than any I had ever before seen.

I do not know whether or not it was because my mind was running so much upon the pirates and upon the great treasure which I had in my keeping, but I am free to say that I liked the looks of the strange craft as little as any I had ever beheld in my life, and would have given a hundred guineas to be safe away from where I was, and with no more favor than a good open sea and a smart breeze, for the *Cassandra* was a first-rate sailer, and as good a ship as any the East India Company had at their docks.

As it was, we were cooped up in what was little more than a pond, and I did not like the looks of the business at all.

"What do you make her out to be, Mr. Langely?" said I, after a bit, handing him the glass.

He took a long and careful look at the stranger. without speaking for a while. By-

and-by he said, without taking his eye from the glass, and as though speaking half to himself, "She's making way against the current somehow or other."

"Yes," said I; "I saw that from the first. But what do you make of her?"

"I can make nothing of her," says he, after a little while.

"Neither can I," I said; "and I like her none the better for that."

Mr. Langely took his eye from the glass, and gave me a very significant look, whereby I saw that he had very much the same notion concerning the stranger that I myself entertained.

By this time there was considerable bustle aboard the *Greenwich*, which rode at anchor not more than a furlong or two from where we lay, and by the gathering of the men on the forecastle I could see that they had sighted the craft, as we had already done.

So the afternoon passed until six o'clock

had come, against which time the stranger had almost come into open sight beyond the cape to the south, the hull alone being hidden by the low spit of sand which formed the extremity of the point.

That evening I took my supper along with the passengers, as I had been used to do, for I wished to appear unconcerned, as, after all, my suspicions might be altogether groundless. Nevertheless, I came upon deck again as soon as I was able, and found that the stranger was now so far come into sight as to show a part of her hull, which was low, and painted black, and was of such an appearance as rather to increase than to lessen my serious suspicions of her nature.

I could see there were two whale-boats ahead of her, and it was very plain to me that it was by means of these that the bark was making head against the current. At first I was more than ever amazed at this, seeing that the current at that point could not run at less than the rate of two or three knots an hour, against which two boats could not hope to tow a craft of her size without some contrivance to aid their efforts. Every now and then I could hear the clicking of the capstan, as though the vessel was heaving anchor, and led by this sound, I after a while perceived how she was making way, though if I had not seen the same plan used in the Strait of Malacca by the *City of Worcester*, when I was there in the year '17, I much misdoubt whether I could have so readily discovered the design which they were in this instance using. As it was, I was not long in finding out what they were about.

The two boats ahead of the strange craft were towing a square sail through the water by a line fastened to the middle of the same. From all four corners of this sail ran good stout ropes, which were made fast to the anchor cable of the bark. The two boats might tow this square through the water easily enough by that one line fastened to the middle, because the sail would then close and so slip easily through the water; but so soon as the bark began to haul upon it from all four corners it spread out as though filled with wind, and so offered a vast resistance to the water. By this contrivance the bark was making headway at about the rate of a knot an hour against the current, so that by seven o'clock she was clear out beyond the cape and into the open water beyond.

At that time the sun had not yet gone down, and the distant vessel stood out against the reddish-gray sky to the eastward, with all the cordage and the masts as sharp as so many hairs and straws in the red light of the setting sun.

I was standing just under the poop-deck at the time, with the glass to my eye, when, of a sudden, I saw something black begin rising from the deck to the fore. There was not enough breeze going to spread it, but I knew as well as anything in all of my life that it was the "Black Roger," and that the white that I could see among the folds was the wicked sign of the "skull and cross-bones," which those bloody and cruel wretch-es are pleased to adopt as the ensign of their trade. Nor were we long in doubt as to their design, for even as I watched I saw a sudden puff of white smoke go up from her side and hang motionlessly in the still air, whilst a second or two later sounded the dull and heavy boom of the distant cannon, and a round shot came skipping across the water from wave to wave, though too far away and with too poor aim to do any damage from that distance, which could not have been less than two miles.

"What does that mean, captain?" said Mistress Pamela, who stood with the other passengers observing the bark from the poop-deck above.

"A salute, madam," said I, and so shut my glass and went into my cabin, where Mr. Langely presently joined me at my request, and where we talked over this very ugly piece of business at our leisure.

V.

In those hot latitudes, such as Madagascar, the darkness cometh very sudden after
sunset, and with no long twilights such as
we have in England, so that within half an
hour after the pirate had saluted us with a
round shot, as told above, it had passed from
daylight to night-time, and there being no
moon until about four o'clock in the morning, it was very dark, with an infinite quantity of stars shining most beautifully in the
sky.

I ordered my gig to be made ready, and
went aboard the *Greenwich*, where I found
Captain Kirby suffering under the utmost
consternation of spirits. He took me straight
to his cabin, where, when we were set down,
he fell to blaming himself most severely for
not having clapped chains upon the fourteen

pirates whom he had found on the island upon his arrival at that place, and who,.it was very plain to see, had given such information to their fellows as had brought a great number of them down upon us.

So soon as I was able I checked him in his self-reproaches. " Come, come, Captain Kirby," says I, " 'tis no time for vain regrets, but rather to be thinking to protect ourselves and those things that we have in trust from these bloody wretches, who would strip us of all."

So, after a while, he quieted in some measure, and the captain of the Ostender coming aboard about this time, we made shift betwixt us to settle some sort of a plan for mutual protection.

According to my suggestions it was determined to get out warps upon the port side of all three crafts, which now lay heading towards the south, because of the set of the current. By means of these warps the vessels might be brought to lie athwart the channel, which was so narrow at this place that, should the pirate craft venture into the harbor, she would be raked by all three in turn. These matters being settled, I returned to the *Cassandra* again.

That night I had but little sleep, but was in and out of my cabin continually. Whenever I was upon the deck I could hear the "click, click, click" of the capstan aboard the pirate vessel, sounding more clearly through the dampness of the night than in the daytime. There was still not a breath of air going, and I thought it likely that the pirate intended making her way into the harbor that night, but about three o'clock in the morning the noise of working the capstan ceased, and I fancied that I heard a sound as of dropping anchor, though I could make out nothing through the darkness, even with the night-glass.

Nor was I mistaken in my surmise that the pirate craft had come to anchor, for when the day broke I perceived that she lay

between two and three miles away, just outside of the capes, and directly athwart the
channel, being stayed by warps, broadside
on, as we ourselves were in the harbor, so
as to rake any vessel that should endeavor
to come out, as we might rake any that
would endeavor to come in.

As this day also was very quiet, with not
a breath of wind stirring, I expected that
the pirate would open fire, though at such
a long range. However, this she did not
do, but lay there as though watching us,
and as though to hold us where we were
until some opportunity or other had ri-
pened. And so came the night again, with
nothing more of note having happened than
the day before.

Ever since we had lain at this spot native
canoes (called by the sailors bumboats) had
come from the shore from day to day, laden
with fruit and fresh provisions, which are
most delicious, refreshing luxuries after a
prolonged sea - voyage, such as ours had

been. That day they had come as usual, though there was little humor for bartering with them upon such a serious occasion.

However, I had observed, and not without surprise, that Captain Leach, though he knew the nature of the pirate craft, and the serious situation in our affairs, appeared so little affected by the danger which threatened us that he bought a lot of fresh fruit, as usual, and held a great deal of conversation with one of the natives, who spoke a sort of English which he had picked up from our traders.

I had not thought much of this at the time, although, as I had observed before, it was not without surprise that I beheld what he did; beyond this I reckoned nothing of it, nor would have done so had not matters of the utmost importance afterwards recalled it to my attention.

That night I had no more appetite for sleep than the night before, and finding little rest or ease in my cabin, was up upon deck for most of the time. Though I did not choose just then to hold conversation with my passengers, I noticed that they were all upon deck, where they sat talking together in low tones. As the night advanced, however, they betook themselves to their cabins, one after another, until only Captain Leach was left sitting alone.

He remained there for maybe the space of half an hour, without moving a hair's-breadth, so far as I could see. At the end of about that length of time, being in a mightily anxious state, I stepped forward to see for myself that the watch was keeping a sharp lookout. I was not gone for more than a minute or two, but when I came back I saw that Captain Leach was no longer where he had been before; yet although I noticed this circumstance at the time, I gave no more thought to it than I would upon an ordinary occasion.

As there was no one on the poop, I myself went up upon that deck, it being so much cooler there than on the quarter-deck below. I took out my pipe and filled it, thinking to have a quiet smoke, which is a most efficacious manner of soothing any perturbation or fermentation of spirits. Just as I was about to strike my flint for a light, I heard a noise under the stern-sheets, as of some one stepping into a boat, and almost immediately afterwards a slight splash, as of an oar or a paddle dipped into the water. I ran hastily to the side of the vessel, and looked astern and into the water below.

Although the sky was clear, the night was excessively dark, as one may often see it in those tropical latitudes; yet I was as well assured that a boat of some sort had left the ship as if I had seen it in broad daylight, because of the phosphorescent trail which it left behind it in its wake.

I had slipped a pistol into my belt before quitting my cabin, and as I hailed the boat I drew it and cocked it, for I thought that the whole occurrence was of a mightily sus-

4

picious nature. As I more than half expected, I got no answer. " Boat, ahoy !" I
cried out a second time, and then, almost
immediately, levelled my pistol and fired,
for I saw that whoever the stranger was,
he had no mind to give me an answer.

At the report of the pistol both Mr.
Langely and Mr. White came running to
where I was, and I explained the suspicious circumstances to them, whereupon
Mr. Langely suggested that it might have
been a shark that I had seen, vast quanti-
ties of which voracious animals dwell in
those and the neighboring waters. I did
not controvert what he said, although I
knew beyond a doubt that it was a craft of
some sort which I had discovered—possibly
a canoe, for the dip of the paddle, which I
had distinctly seen in the phosphorescence
of the water, appeared first upon the one
side of the wake and then upon the other,
as the blade was dipped into the water from
side to side ; so although, as I said, I did not

undertake to controvert Mr. Langely's opinion, I was mightily discomposed in my own
mind concerning the business.

At this time there was a vast deal of dis-
turbance aboard the *Greenwich* and the Ostender because of my hail and the discharge
of the pistol, which, however, soon quieted
down when they found that nothing further
followed upon the alarm.

I walked up and down the poop-deck for
a great while, endeavoring to conceive what
could be the meaning of the boat, which
had most undoubtedly been lying under the
stern of the *Cassandra*, and how it came
that the watch had failed so entirely to discover its arrival. It would not have been
possible for an ordinary ship's boat to come
upon us so undiscovered, for, as I myself
knew, the watch were keeping a sharper
lookout than usual; therefore this circumstance, together with that which I had above
observed concerning my opinion that the
craft had been rowed with a paddle, led me

to conclude that it was one of the native canoes, though I was as far as ever from guessing what the object of the visit had been, or what it portended. As I sat ruminating upon this subject, looking straight ahead of me, without thinking whither my observation was directed, I presently perceived that I was looking absently at the spot where Captain Leach had been sitting a little while before. This led me to think of him, and from him of the jewel that was in my keeping, and of its excessive value. Of a sudden it flashed into my mind, as quick as lightning, what if Captain Leach should have it in his mind to practice some treachery upon us all?

I may truly say that this thought would never have entered my brains had not the circumstance of Captain Leach's conversation with me in my cabin tended to set it there. But no sooner had this gloomy suspicion found place in my mind than it and those troubles which had beset me of late, and the loss of that sleep which I had failed to enjoy the night before, together cast me into such a ferment of spirits as I hope I may never again experience. Nor could I reason my mind out of what I could not but feel might be insane and unreasonable fancyings.

At last I could bear my uncertainties no longer, but went down into the great cabin, and so to the door of the berth which Captain Leach occupied. I knocked softly upon the door, and then waited a while, but received no answer. After that I knocked again, and louder, but with no better success than before. Finding I was like to have no answer to my knocking, I tried the door, and found that it was locked.

My heart began to beat at a great rate at all this; but I suddenly bethought me that perhaps the captain was a sound sleeper and not easily roused. If this were so, and he were in his cabin, and had locked the door upon himself, I could easily convince

myself of the fact, for it hardly could be
doubted but that the key would be in the
key-hole. I drew out my pocket-knife,
opened a small blade which it contained,
and thrust it into the key-hole. There was
no key there!

This discovery acted upon my spirits in
such a manner that a douse of water could
not have cooled me quicker; for now that
my worst suspicions were so far confirmed
—for I felt well assured that Captain Leach
was nowhere aboard the ship—my perturbation left me, and I grew of a sudden as
calm as I am at this very moment. However, to make matters more assured, I rapped
again upon the door of the cabin, and this
time with more vigor than before; but although I repeated the knocking four or five
times, I received no answer, and so went upon
deck to consider the matter at my leisure.

My first thought was of the jewel in my
keeping, and that Captain Leach had made
off with it. My cooler reason told me that

this could not be, I having taken such effectual means to hide it, as before stated. Nevertheless, I went to my cabin and examined my hiding-place to set my mind at rest, finding, as might be expected, that the jewel was safely there.

My first impulse was to tell Mr. Langely of my suspicions, but in digesting the matter it appeared to me best to keep them to myself for the present; for if I should, after all, prove wrong in my surmise, it would only add to the entanglement to have another involved in the business before anything certain had been discovered; moreover, should I observe sufficient cause for using extreme measures against Captain Leach, I might easily arrest him at any time, having him entirely in my power.

Having settled this matter to my own satisfaction, I determined to lie in wait for his return, and to discover how he himself would explain his absence.

I surmised that he must have left the ship

from the boat which was hanging to the davits astern, and on inspecting the matter, found that I was correct, and that a stout line, such as might easily bear the weight of a man, had been lashed to one of the falls, and hung to within a foot or two of the water. I was then well assured that Captain Leach must have clambered into the boat astern whilst I had gone forward, as told above, and had dropped thence into the canoe by means of the line just spoken of. The noise which I had heard I conceived to have been caused by his making a misstep, or by the canoe rising with the ground - swell more than he had expected.

Now, if he left the ship in that manner, of which, according to my mind, there could be but little doubt, there was equal certainty that he would return by the same way; so I determined to lie in watch for him there, and to tax him with his absence so soon as he should come aboard. Accordingly I laid myself down in the boat astern as comfortably as I could contrive, and lighting my pipe, watched with all the patience I could command for the return of the fugitive.

I judge that I lay there for the space of two or three hours, and in all that time saw or heard nothing to arouse my suspicions; nor do I believe that I would have discovered anything had I not been watching at that very place, for so quiet was Captain Leach's return that I heard no sound of oars nor knew anything of it until I saw the line that hung at the davits moved from below by some one climbing aboard. I lay perfectly still and made no noise until he had clambered into the boat and stood within a few feet of me.

"Well, sir," says I, as quietly as I could speak, "and may I ask where you have been for all this long time?"

VI.

Had a pistol been fired beside his head he could not have started more violently, and I had thought that he would have been utterly dumfounded; but he recovered himself with a most amazing quickness.

"Why, Captain Mackra," says he, with a laugh, "and is it you that welcome me back again, like the prodigal that I am?"

"Sir," said I, very sternly, "you will be pleased to answer my question, for I tell you plain that I am in no humor for jesting upon this occasion."

"And why should I not jest?" says he; "the whole business is a jest from first to last. As all this coil has been made about a very simple piece of business, I am forced to tell what I had not intended to tell, and which I am surprised that a man of your feeling should urge another into declaring. A man of parts, sir, may find favor with dusky beauties as well as with white; nor can I see what more harm there may be in visiting a sweetheart here than at Gravesend, which I doubt not you yourself have done, and that more than once."

I confess that I was vastly struck aback at this reasonable answer, and began for a moment to misdoubt that my suspicions of the captain were correct. For a while I stood, not knowing what to say, when of a sudden certain circumstances struck me that Captain Leach's words had not explained.

"And why," said I, "at a time of such anxiety and uncertainty, did you not ask permission to leave the ship?"

"I should think," says he, "a man of delicacy would have no need to ask such a question as that."

"Then tell me this," I cried, "*why did you not direct your course towards the land instead of towards the open sea?*"

" Why," says he, laughing, and answering
with the utmost readiness, " I thought of
nothing at all but of getting away from the
ship as fast as possible, seeing that some
hasty fool aboard was blazing away at me
with a pistol or musquetoon, and that if I
had been picking my course at the time I
might have wound up the business with an
ounce of lead in my brains, instead of en-
joying this pleasant conversation in such
good health."

All this time we had been standing within a foot or two of one another, I looking
him straight in the face, though I could see
nothing of it in the darkness. For a moment or two I could make no answer, his
words being so mightily plausible; and yet
I did not believe a single one of them, for
they ran so smoothly and glibly that I could
not but feel convinced that he had them
already sorted and arranged for just such
an occasion as the present.

" Sir," said I, in a low voice, for I was

afraid lest my indignation should get the better of me, " I tell you plain that, though your words are so smooth, I do not believe that which you tell me. Go to your cabin, sir, and let me tell you that if I see anything that may tend to confirm my suspicions of you, I will clap you in irons, without waiting a second, and as sure as you are a living man."

" Captain Mackra," said he, in a voice as quiet as that I myself had used, "if ever I come safely to land, you shall answer to me for these words, sir."

" That as you please," said I ; and thereupon turned and left the boat, entering my own cabin so soon as I had seen that Captain Leach had obeyed my orders by betaking himself to his.

I was not thus quickly to see the last of this part of the affair, for early the next morning, and before I had left my cabin, Mr. Langely comes to me with a message from Captain Leach to the effect that he

would like to have a few words with me. I
at once sent a return message that I would
be pleased to see him at whatever time it
might suit him to come. Accordingly in
about five minutes he knocked upon the
door of my cabin, and I bade him enter. I
motioned him to a chair, but he only bowed
and remained standing where he was, nigh
to the door.

" Captain Mackra," said he, coldly, " you
were pleased to put upon me last night a
gross and uncalled-for insult. I cannot sum-
mon you to account for it at present, although I hope to do so in the future. But
you may perceive, sir, that it will be best
both for you and for myself that I should
withdraw from this ship, and finish my passage to India, as the opportunity now offers,
either in the *Greenwich* or the *Van Wei-
land*" (which was the name of the Ostend
boat).

I was overjoyed at so propitious an opportunity of getting thus easily rid of my

"CAPTAIN MACKRA," SAID HE, COLDLY, "YOU WERE PLEASED TO PUT UPON ME LAST NIGHT A GROSS AND UNCALLED-FOR INSULT."

uncomfortable passenger. However, I think I showed nothing of this to him—at least I endeavored not to do so—and told him that a boat was at his service if he chose to look for another berth for the rest of the voyage. I myself went upon deck and had the gig lowered, into which Captain Leach presently stepped, having bid good-by to his fellow-passengers, and having said that he would send for his chest so soon as he had secured a berth in one or the other of the vessels mentioned. I gave directions to the boat-swain, who was captain of the gig, to await Captain Leach's orders until he should indicate that he had no further use for the boat, and then saw him rowed away to the *Greenwich* with the most inexpressible pleasure.

The *Cassandra's* boat lay alongside of the *Greenwich* for maybe half an hour, at the end of which time I was surprised to see Captain Leach re-enter her, and direct his course to the Ostender, which lay a little

distance beyond. He remained aboard of
her for about the same length of time that
he had stayed with the *Greenwich*, after
which he climbed the boat for a third time,
and directed his course for the *Cassandra*
again.

I was standing upon the quarter-deck
when he came aboard, and he approached
me with a countenance expressive of the utmost mortification and chagrin.

"Captain Mackra," said he, "I find that
by a most unfortunate sequence of events I
can find a berth neither aboard the *Greenwich* nor the Ostender, so that nothing re-
mains but for me to force my unwelcome
presence upon you for the balance of the
voyage."

I own that I was very much disappointed by these words. However, nothing remained but to put the best face possible
upon the matter. "Sir," said I, as gracious-
ly as I could contrive to speak, although I
am afraid that my tone was expressive of

my disappointment, "it was at your own suggestion that you quitted the *Cassandra;* your berth, sir, is still ready for your occupation."

He said nothing further, but indicating his acknowledgments with a bow, proceeded directly to his cabin.

5

VII.

As I was in such a ferment of spirit for all this time, and so fearful of an attack from the pirate craft, having continually in my mind not only the treasure, but also the helpless women intrusted to my keeping, it might occur to the reader to ask why I did not send both it and them to such a place of safety upon the land as the king's town offered to English people beset as we were. I may now say that I had considered it, and had perceived that more than one difficulty lay in the way. In the first place, I could not send the ship's boat to the king's town, because that in passing the cape to the northward they would come within a mile or less of the pirate craft, from which they might not hope to escape without molestation.

Secondly, I could not send them across the country, because it would require not only an escort such as could be ill spared at this juncture, but also an efficient leader, who might be spared even less readily. Besides this, I could not tell what dangers such a party might encounter, not only from natives, of whose disposition I knew nothing, but also from wild beasts, which we could hear distinctly every night, howling in the jungles in a most melancholy, dreadful manner.

Thirdly and lastly, I did not believe the pirates would stay long where they were, as I had often heard of the cowardly disposition of these bloody wretches; wherefore I hoped that, seeing how well we were posted to guard ourselves against an attack from them, they might take themselves away upon the first occasion, which they could not now do because of the calm weather. I furthermore argued that in any event, should occasion render it necessary,

I could easily disembark my passengers with but little loss of time, and as easily and safely then as now.

Such had been the nature of my thoughts whenever I had directed them upon the melancholy and gloomy state of our affairs. Yet had the most sinister forebodings which I had entertained at those times been fulfilled, our misfortunes could not have equalled those which in truth fell upon us, the history of which I have immediately to tell.

Captain Leach's trip in search of a new berth had been undertaken so early in the morning that it was not yet noon when he had returned. Some little time after that, I being in my own cabin at the time, there came of a sudden a sound that was, as it were, the first muttering of the storm that was so soon to fall upon us. It was the dull and heavy boom of a single cannon, sounding from a great way off, and which I instantly knew had been fired aboard of the pirate craft.

I went straight upon the deck, where I found the weather still as dead a calm as it had been the two days before, with not so much as a breath of air stirring or a cat's-paw upon the water. The ground-swell rose and fell as smoothly as though the sea ran with oil instead of water, and the sky above had an appearance as of a solid sheet of steel-blue, with not so much as one single cloud upon the whole face of it. But the first thing that I beheld was the pirate craft, and that they were hoisting sail as though they perceived a breeze coming, of which we saw nothing. Across her port bow the smoke of her gun still hung like a round white cloud just above the glassy surface of the sea.

"Sure she means to quit us, Mr. Langely," said I; but Mr. Langely never answered, for just as he opened his lips to speak, the lookout roared, "Sail ho!"

"Where away?" sang out Mr. White, who was officer of the deck at that time.

But before the word reached us I myself, and I suspect most of the others, had sighted the craft away to the southward, coming up under full sail, and with a breeze of which we could see nothing.

She was at that time some six or seven miles distant, and just emerging from be‑ hind a raised thicket of scrub bushes that lay betwixt her and the *Cassandra*, and which had hidden her until now.

The strange craft was a large sloop, of such an appearance that even had not thê pirate fired that which was no doubt a sig‑ nal-gun, methinks I should have entertained the most sinister and gloomy forebodings concerning her nature and her character.

" What do you think of her, Mr. Langely?" said I, after watching her for some time in silence.

" It is the pirate's consort, sir," said he, very seriously.

' . " I do believe you are right," said I, " and that is why she has been waiting for all these days, keeping us bottled up so that we could not have got away even if we had had a breeze."

I did not tell Mr. Langely all that was upon my mind; nevertheless, I could not but regard our present position as one of the most extreme peril. For if one pirate craft, with its crew of blood-thirsty wretches, was a match for us sufficient to hold us where we now were, what harm might not two of them accomplish should they attack us peaceful merchantmen, unused as we were to the arts of war, in this narrow harbor, where we might hope neither to manœuvre nor to escape.

We were already cleared for action, having had full time to prepare ourselves since danger had first threatened us; accordingly, leaving Mr. Langely to supervise such few details as might still remain to demand attention, I had my gig lowered, and went aboard of the *Greenwich* to consult with Captain Kirby as to means of defending ourselves against this new and additional danger that threatened our existence.

The Ostend captain was there when I came aboard, and I fancied, though I then knew not why, that he and Captain Kirby looked at one another in a very strange and peculiar manner when I entered the cabin. Besides that, I noticed little or no preparation for action had been made.   ·

"We'll stand by you," says Captain Kirby; "in course we'll stand by you, though you must know it is each one for himself, and devil take the hindmost, at such times as these."

I was mightily amazed and taken aback at this speech. "And why do you talk so about standing by me, Captain Kirby?" said I. "Is it not, then, that we stand by one another? Is my craft in greater peril than yours, or am I to be given up as a sacrifice to these wicked and bloody wretches?"

I thought he seemed vastly disturbed at this speech.

" In course," says he, " we'll stand by one another. All the same, each must look out for himself."

I regarded Captain Kirby for a while without speaking, and he seemed more than ever troubled at my gaze.

" Sir! sir!" I cried, " I must tell you that I do not understand this matter. Do you not mean to make a fight of it?"

At this he flew into a mighty fume. " How!" says he; " do you mean to question my courage? Do you call me a coward?"

" No, sir," says I, " I call you nothing; only I did not understand your speech. Sure, sir, you cannot but remember that I have three helpless women aboard my ship, and that it behooves you as a man and an Englishman to stand by me in this time of peril."

So saying, I left the cabin and the ship, but with the weight of trouble that lay upon my mind anything but lightened, for

I could not understand why, we all being in this peril together, neither he nor the Ostend captain had spoken a single word concerning our defence.

However, I yet retained the hope that the pirates would not venture into our harbor, seeing that we were three to two, and lying in a chosen position whence we might hope to defend ourselves for a long time, and to their undoing.

Upon my return I found my passengers all in the great cabin, and in a very serious mood, having heard some rumor as to the danger that threatened. I stood for a while as though not knowing what to say, but at last I made shift to tell them how matters stood, and in what danger we were like to be, though I smoothed everything over as much as lay in my power. I think that our peril had been pretty well discussed amongst them before I confirmed it with that which I said. Nevertheless, I am amazed even now at the coolness with which all hands regarded it.

Mistress Pamela, I recollect, laid her hand lightly upon my arm. "Whatever our danger may be," she cried, "this we all know, that we could confide our safety to no truer sailor nor more gallant man than he who commands this ship." This she said before them all who were there standing.

In my cabin I summoned Mr. Langely and Mr. White (my second mate) to a serious consultation, which was the last we were to hold before that great and bloody battle concerning which so much hath been writ and spoken of late. When we had finished our councils we came upon deck again, and found that the sloop was rather less than a mile distant from the other craft, and in a little while she hove to nigh to the barque, and let go her anchor with a splash and rattle of the cable which we could hear distinctly whence we lay.

For half an hour Mr. Langely and I stood

·upon the poop-deck watching the two crafts by aid of the telescope, and what we saw in that time foreboded to my mind no good to ourselves.

First we beheld a boat pass from the barque to the sloop, and in which was one evidently of great consequence amongst the pirates, for by aid of the glass we could distinguish that his apparel was better than the others, and also that he wore what appeared to be a crimson scarf tied about his body.

He remained aboard the sloop for maybe the space of ten minutes, at the end of which time he returned again to the barque, where they immediately began lowering away the boats. Four of these boats were filled with men who were all transported to the sloop, up the side of which we soon saw them swarm to the number of fifty or more.

Whilst these things had been going forward, Mr. Langely and I had been standing in silence, but now my first mate turned to me, "Sir," said he, "methinks that they mean to attack us."

I nodded my head in answer, but said nothing.

By this time the breeze was wellnigh upon us, for the smooth water all around us was dusked by the little cat's-paws that swept the glassy surface.

Now that morning, just before the pirate sloop hove in sight, I had got out warps by means of which I hoped to change our position, bringing the *Cassandra* nigher to the *Greenwich*, and to a station of greater defence. In this, however, we had made but little progress, for the current set strong against us at the present state of the tide. Seeing now the imminence of the attack, I hoisted sail, hoping to take advantage of the first wind, and bring the *Cassandra* closer to the *Greenwich*.

What followed I am even now not able to explain, for I am slow to believe that one

English captain could desert another in
such an emergency as the present. It might
be that Captain Kirby thought that we intended trying to get away upon the wind,
for the *Greenwich* also began immediately
to set all her sail. Seeing what they were
about I hailed the other craft, but got no
answer. Then I hailed her again and again,
but still received no reply.

The next minute she, being open to the
first puffs of the breeze by a valley, filled
and bore away, followed by the Ostender,
who had also set her sails, leaving me becalmed where I was.

" My God !" cried Mr. Langely, " do they
mean to desert us? Look, sir, here come
the pirates !"

I had just then been so intent upon the
other vessels that I had not thought of observing what our enemies were about, not
thinking that they would take such immediate action. But, no doubt, seeing us set
our sails, and fearing that we might get

away, slipped their own cables; for they were now coming down upon us with the freshening wind, having already entered the channel as boldly as though there were none to oppose them, the sloop leading the others by a quarter of a mile or so. Indeed the *Greenwich* and the Ostender bearing away had left the passage entirely open to them, with no one but ourselves to oppose them.

In this extremity I hailed the *Greenwich* for a third time, and getting no answer, ordered the gunner to fire across her bows, but in spite of this she did not heave to, whereupon we gave her a round shot, but whether to her harm or no I am not able to say.

And now nothing remained for us but to fight what appeared a hopeless battle against heavy odds.

The main ship-channel leading from the offing to the bay or harbor wherein the

Cassandra, the *Greenwich*, and the Ostender had been riding for these days past, lead almost easterly and westerly, but so shaped by the sand-bars to the south and those shoals that ran out from the northern cape as to take the form of a very crooked letter S.   Nowhere was this channel over half or three-quarters of a mile wide, and in some places it was hardly more than a quarter of a mile wide.

From the position which the *Cassandra* occupied this entrance to the harbor was so well defended that any vessel entering thereat must be twice raked by our broadside fire, once in rounding the northern, and once the southern angle of the channel. Hence it was that I determined to hold our present position as long as I was able.

But the pirates did not both attack us by way of the main ship-channel as we had expected, for when they had rounded the northern angle the sloop, fearing perhaps that we would try to get away upon the wind, instead of keeping in consort with the barque, made directly for us across the shoals that lay between us and them. This they were able to do without running aground, both because of their intimate knowledge of these intricate waters and of the small amount of water which the sloop drew.

"We'll rake 'em anyhow," says I to Mr. Langely, for I could see no other means for them to approach us but to come upon us bow on, there being no room to manœuvre among the bars and shoals that lay betwixt us and them.

But the devilish ingenuity of these cruel, wicked wretches supplied them with other means than a direct attack upon the *Cassandra*, for, when they had come within about a mile or so of us, they hove to, dropped their main-sail, and, running out great oars from the ports between decks, began rowing towards us in a clumsy fashion, somewhat after the man-

6

ner of a galleon. By this means, and by the aid of the current which set towards us, they were enabled to keep nearly broadside on, and so avoid being raked by our fire.

"Mr. Langely," said I, "if they are able to board us we are lost. Order the gunner to fire upon the oars and not upon the decks."

"Ay, ay," says he, and turned away.

VIII.

THE pirates were the first to open the battle, which they did when within about a quarter of a mile from us, giving us a broadside. It was the first time that I had ever been under fire in all of my life, and never shall I forget it as long as I may live. Their aim was wonderfully accurate, so that when their shot struck us a great cloud of white splinters flew from a dozen places at once. I saw three men drop upon the deck, and one who stood at a gun on the quarter-deck just below me leaned suddenly forward half across the cannon with a deep groan, whilst a fountain of blood gushed out from his bosom across the carriage and upon the deck. One of the others caught him by the arm, whereupon he turned half round and then slipped and fell forward upon his face.

He was the first man killed in this action, and the first that I ever beheld die in a like manner.

The *Cassandra* answered the pirate's fire almost immediately. But our guns were trained, as I had ordered, upon the oars and not upon the crowded decks, so that while every shot that they delivered told upon the lives of the poor fellows aboard the *Cassandra*, our return fire did apparently no harm to them.

I hope I may never again feel such an agony of impatience and doubt and almost despair, as I beheld my men fall by ones and twos upon the deck, which soon became stained and smeared with their blood whilst the pirate craft came drifting ever nigher and nigher to us, its decks swarming with yelling, naked wretches that in their aspect and manners resembled demons incarnated rather than mortal men.

" Mr. Langely," said I, in a low voice, " if those oars are not broken in five minutes' time we are all lost." For there yet remained three thrust through the ports upon the side nighest to the *Cassandra*, and the current was carrying the pirate craft in such a direction that if they were able to hold their course a little while longer they would be almost certain to drift upon us and so board us.

One minute passed, and two minutes, then there was a shiver of splinters, and only one oar was left. Instantly the stern of the sloop began to swing slowly around towards us, for one oar was not enough to keep her to the current. I could see the ash wood bend with the strain like a willow twig, then—snap!—it broke, and around came the stern with a swing directly under our fire. The pirates sprang to the main-sheets, but it was too late to save themselves.

When the crew of the *Cassandra* saw the result of their fire they burst out shouting and cheering like madmen. Down came the sloop drifting stern on, whilst the *Cassandra*, making up for lost time, poured broadside after broadside into her. Never did I behold such a sight in all of my life, for every shot we gave her ploughed great lanes along her crowded decks. To make matters worse for them, their mast was presently shot through, falling alongside in a great tangled wreck, thus preventing any manœuvres which they might still have hoped to make. They drifted by us at about forty or fifty yards' distance, shouting and yelling, and giving us a last broadside with great courage and determination. They presently ran aground upon a sandbar and there stuck fast for the time, though in such shoal water that we could not come nigher to them than we then were.

All this while the barque had been slowly making her way through the tortuous turnings of the channel. At one point, the water being low, she had run aground, and

though she had cleared again with the rising
tide, she had been so delayed by this mis-
chance that she had not been able to come
up in aid of her consort.

But immediately they discerned what mis-
hap had befallen the sloop, and that she
was fast aground and in no present position
to attack us, they hove to and lay directly
athwart the channel.

I at once perceived their intentions, and
that they were determined to keep us shut
up where we were until the sloop could float
clear away with the rising tide and resume
her attack against us. It was then that the
resolve entered my mind not to await an attack but to seek it ourselves; for though the
crew of the barque must have outnumbered
that of the *Cassandra* two to one, she was
yet much the smaller vessel of the two and
the less heavily armed. Now, if we could
only once get past her and safe into the
channel our safety would be wellnigh assured; for, as said above, the *Cassandra*

was one of the best sailers at the East India
Company's docks.

I turned and beckoned my first mate to
me. "Sir," said I, "yonder is our one and
only chance of getting away; we must run
down upon that vessel in the channel, en-
gage her, and trust to God and take our
chance of getting safe past her and away.
If we are fortunate enough to pass her we
can gain a good start before she can round
to in such narrow sea-room." Mr. Langely opened his mouth as though to speak.
"Nay, nay, sir," I cried, "it is our only
chance, and we *must* take it."

At first we did not suffer so much as I
had expected from the fire of the pirate; but
when we had come within one hundred or
two hundred yards of them, and when within range of the musketry in their fore and
main tops, their fire was truly dreadful.

The *Cassandra's* wheel was stationed under the overhang of the poop-deck, and upon

the helmsman most of their aim was concentrated; for if the *Cassandra* was once allowed to fall off, and should run aground in the narrow channel, she would then be in their power, and they could destroy her at their leisure.

One after another three men fell at that dangerous post, which was entirely open to the pirate's fire. We were now within one hundred and fifty yards of them, and a fourth took hold, but only for a minute, for he presently dropped upon his knees, though he still kept a tight grip on the wheel, keeping the ship upon her course. Mr. Langely and I were standing under the overhang of the poop, whereupon he, seeing that the man was wounded, without waiting for orders from me, sprang forward and seized the wheel in his own hands just as the other fell forward upon his face.

The next minute Mr. Langely cried out, " My God, captain, I am shot!" His right hand fell at his side, and in an instant I beheld his shirt stained with blood that gushed out from the wound in his shoulder.

The ship beginning to fall off, I ran forward and took the wheel myself, for in a minute more, if we held our course, we would be under the pirate's stern, and in a position to rake them with our starboard broadside. I heard a dozen bullets strike into the wood-work around me; one struck the wheel, so that I felt as if my hand and my wrist were paralyzed by the jar. The next instant I felt a terrible blow upon my head; a hot red stream gushed over my face and into my eyes, and for a moment my brain reeled. Some one caught hold of me, but just as darkness settled upon me I felt the ship shake beneath me and heard the roar of our broadside. We were under the pirate's stern at last.

I could not have lain insensible for many minutes, for when I opened my eyes and saw the surgeon and my second mate bend-

ing over me, it was still with the roar of
cannon in my ears.

"How is this, Mr. White?" cried I; "are
we not then past the pirate?"

"Sir," said my second mate, in a very serious voice, "we are run aground."

"And the pirate?" cried I.

"She is also aground," said he, "and we
rake her with every shot."

I got to my feet, in spite of the surgeon's
protest, putting him impatiently aside.

It was as Mr. White said; the pirate was
aground about two or three hundred yards
away from us, fast stuck upon the bar, stern
towards us. She must have received more
than one shot betwixt wind and water, for
she was heeled over to one side, and I could
see a stream of bloody water pouring continually from her scupper-holes.

But I also saw that we were stuck hard
and fast, and that though our position was
better than theirs, every shot that we fired
drove us with the recoil more firmly aground.

I at once gave orders that all firing except with muskets should be stopped; so there we lay aground for more than half an hour, answering the pirate's fire with our flintlocks.

Although this was dreadful for us to bear at the time, in the end it proved to be our salvation; for when the tide raised we floated clear fully ten minutes before the pirates, and so escaped immediate destruction.

In the mean time, whilst we lay there the sloop had floated clear, and the pirates having cut away the wreck of the main-mast, and having rigged up oars like those we had shot away, presently came to the aid of their consort. Seeing our situation, and that we were fast aground, they did not attack us directly, but made for the channel by the way which they had left it, thus entering above us and cutting off all our chance of escape. For though we had so nearly passed the other craft, we could not hope to pass them without being boarded, for with their oars they could come as they chose, and were not dependent on the wind.

So soon as they had entered the channel they laid their course directly for us, but before they could come up with us, we also had floated clear, as before stated; and though we could not escape to the open water, we were yet enabled to enter the harbor again, which we did, followed by the fire of the pirate barque.

The wind now had almost fallen away again, so that the sloop, driven by her oars, and enabled by her light draught to cross the shoals and bars which we could not make, began to draw up with us, endeavoring with all diligence to board us. Nevertheless, we contrived to make a running fight of it for almost an hour.

At last, the other vessel having repaired her damages, and having some time since floated clear off, came down upon us in aid of her consort, for the sloop was very plainly filling rapidly, having heeled over so much to one side that her decks were greatly exposed to our fire.

For all this long time the *Greenwich* and Ostender had been riding at about three or four miles distant, not being able to escape to open water whilst the pirates held the channel. But so far from coming to our assistance, they made no sign of help or fired so much as a single gun in our aid.

By this time more than half of my officers and men had been either killed or wounded, so that when I beheld the barque, crowded with naked, howling wretches, thirsting for our blood, come bearing down upon us, and when I beheld how little hope there was of Captain Kirby's coming to our assistance, I could see no other chance for our safety than to run the *Cassandra* ashore, and, if possible, to escape to the beach as best we could. Accordingly, I gave the necessary orders to Mr. White, and the *Cassandra* laid her course for the beach, closely followed only by the pirate barque, the sloop having already been run ashore about half a mile below to keep her from sinking.

In five minutes the *Cassandra* struck, grounding at about fifty yards from the shore. The pirate drew fully four feet less water, but it pleased God that she stuck fast on higher ground, so that, after all, they were prevented from boarding us.

Here we fought, for nearly an hour, the last, and I know not whether it was not the bloodiest engagement of that whole day; nor can I sufficiently praise the behavior not only of the officers, but of the men, who even in this extremity behaved with the most extraordinary courage, though the crew of the sloop supplied the larger vessel with three boatfuls of fresh men.

Meantime the *Greenwich* followed the lead of the Ostender and stood clear away to sea, leaving us struggling in the very jaws of death. Soon after the pirate craft floated clear off with the rising tide, and immediately fell to work fitting out warps to haul out under our stern, though still at some distance from us.

Seeing this, no hope remained for us but to leave the ship, if possible, with the passengers and such of our men as were still alive, trusting to Providence not only to bring us safe away, but to keep us all in that desolate country amongst a strange and savage people.

IX.

As said above, it was now past six o'clock, and Mr. White and the boatswain were the only unwounded officers with whom I dared intrust the command of the boats in executing my plans for leaving the ship.*

The long-boat and the gig were all that remained sound and uninjured, the others having been shot or stove during the engagement. It was arranged that Mr. Jeks, the boatswain, should command the long-boat, and Mr. White the gig. The passengers and the less seriously wounded were to go in the long-boat; Mr. White to take

---

* Mr. Richards, the third mate, had been killed by a grape bullet when we ran down upon the larger of the pirate crafts. He was a young man of great promise, of but twenty-two years of age, and my cousin's son.

7

those who had been more dangerously hurt
in the gig.

By this time the wind had died down
again, and it was as calm as it had been the
two days before, so that the smoke hung
thick about the ship and upon the water,
and did not drift away.   Although, because
of this thick cloud, we could not see our
enemy, and so could not point our guns
with any sureness of aim, it also prevented
him from seeing us and what we were about,
so that all our movements were concealed
from him as his were from us.

Mr. Langely having come upon deck at
this time, though very weak and feeble from
the pain of his wound, I intrusted the clear-
ing away and lowering of the boats to him,
while I went below to advise the women of
our plans, and to tell them to get together
such matters as they might need in this
emergency.   I found them in a most pitiable state, having been sent below at the first
sign of the approaching battle, and left by

themselves for all this long time with no light but that of a lantern slung from the deck above, hearing the uproar of the fight and the groans of the wounded without once knowing whether matters were going for us or against us.

The two ladies sat, or rather crouched, upon a chest or box, holding one another by the hand. Mistress Ann lay huddled in a corner in a most extreme state of terror and distraction.

I may even yet see in my mind's eye how Mistress Pamela appeared when I clambered down the ladder: her face was as white as marble, and her eyes gazed out from the shadow of her brows with a most intense and burning glance. My heart bled for the poor creatures when I thought how much they must have suffered since they were sent to this dreadful place.

So soon as they saw me they fell to screaming, and clung to one another. Nor did I wonder at their distraction when I beheld myself a few minutes later in the glass in my cabin, for my face and hands were blackened with the smoke of the powder, my shirt and waistcoat were stained with the blood which had poured out from the wound in my head, and around my brow was bound a bloody napkin which I had hastily wrapped about my head so soon as I had recovered from the first effects of my wound. But just then I knew not how I looked, nor reckoned anything of it, for in a fight such as we had passed through one has little time to think of such matters.

"Ladies," said I, speaking as gently as I could, "be not afraid ; it is I, Captain Mackra."

At this Mrs. Evans burst into a great passion of weeping, with her face buried in her hands, while Mistress Pamela still regarded me, though with a fixed and stony stare.

"Oh God !" she cried; "and are you hurt?" And she pointed with her outstretched finger to my head.

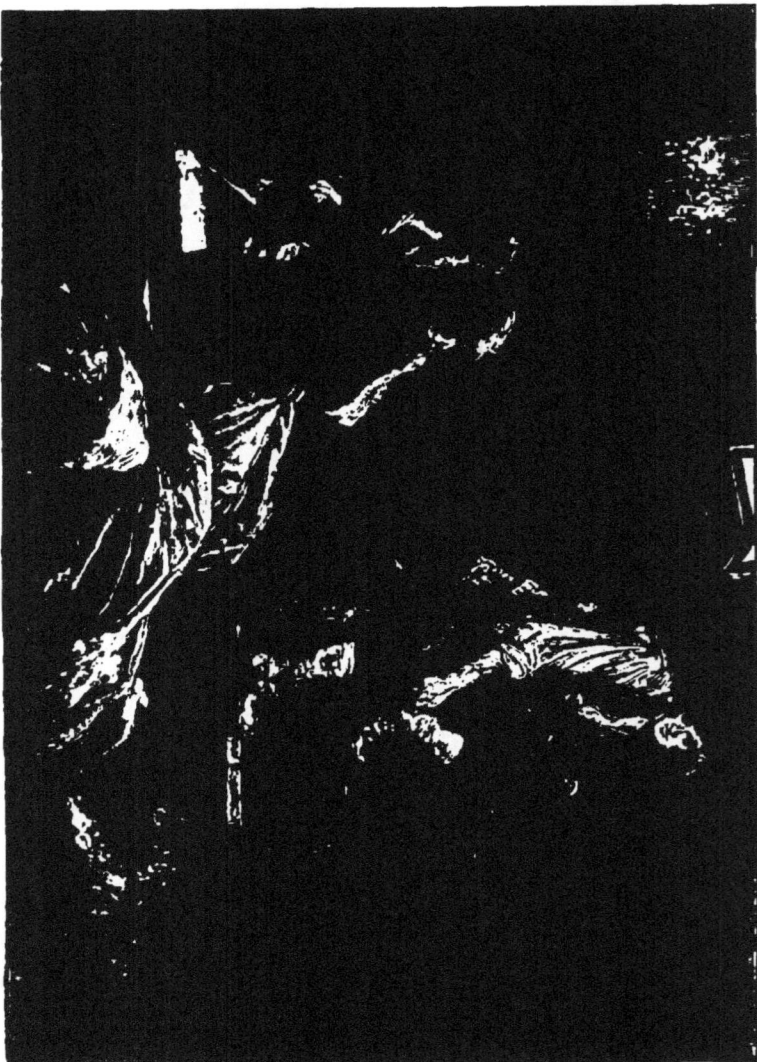

SO SOON AS THEY SAW ME THEY FELL TO SCREAMING, AND CLUNG TO ONE ANOTHER.

"Why, no," says I, making shift to force a laugh in spite of the anxiety with which I was consumed; "it is a mere scratch, and nothing to speak of. There is no time now to talk of such little matters as this, but only of leaving the ship, for we can defend ourselves no longer. Get together what things you need from your cabin, and make haste, for there is no time to lose."

I believe that Mistress Ann had fainted clean away when she had caught sight of me climbing down the ladder, for we found that she was in no condition to move, so I picked her up in my arms and bore her to the great cabin, the others following close behind. There I left them and went again upon deck, where I found that they were bringing the wounded up from below.

I hope I may never see such a sight again to the very last day of my life, for it is one thing to behold a man shot in the heat of an action, and another and a mightily different thing to see one of one's own shipmates carried groaning in a hammock wet and stained with his blood.

We had so grounded that we lay within fifty yards of the shore, and it could take but a little while for a boat to go thither and return to the ship again. Nevertheless, I deemed it necessary to give the Rose of Paradise into the keeping of some one going upon this first passage, and upon whom I could entirely rely. The boatswain had the care of the women, which was, of course, of the first importance of all; therefore, there remained no one in whose hands I could place it with as much confidence as in those of Mr. White.

It was very necessary to keep up the show of fighting, lest the pirates should think we had surrendered, and so come aboard of us, but all hands who could be spared from the guns were engaged in lowering the wounded into the long-boat and gig.

Leaving Mr. Langely in charge of this, I took Mr. White into my cabin; there I opened the locker that I had made in my berth, and took out the box containing the jewel.

"Sir," said I, "I am about to show you a sign both of my regard and of my esteem. In this box is a jewel worth above three hundred thousand pounds; this I intrust for the present into your keeping. When you get to the shore you will not return with the gig, but will remain where you are, sending the boat back under some one whom you may choose among your crew. Should I perish, or should the pirates board this ship before you return (in which event I cannot hope to escape with my life), you will convey this trust to Mr. Longways, the Company's agent at the king's town. And now, sir, I wish you God's speed."

Mr. White was about to reply, but I checked him, telling him that he could best show his regard for me by leaving the ship without further words.

We quitted my cabin together, and just

outside we met Captain Leach, whom I had noticed repeatedly for the last half-hour, and never very far away from me. He came directly towards Mr. White and me, but he did not so much as glance at the box that Mr. White held, but spoke to me.

" I came upon Mistress Pamela Boon's account," said he. " The women are ready to quit the ship, and Mistress Ann is yet in a dead swoon."

" I will go to them," said I; and then turning to Mr. White, I said, very seriously, " Remember!"

He did not answer, but bowed his head, and I turned and left him, Captain Leach following close behind me. He did not enter with me into the great cabin, but waited without, and when I came out a few minutes later I saw that he was gone.

I found the ladies waiting in the cabin, each with a bundle tied up in a kerchief. The waiting-woman lay upon the floor, still in a swoon, with Mistress Pamela kneeling beside her, chafing and slapping her hands, whilst Mrs. Evans sat at the table with her face buried in her palms. So soon as I entered Mistress Pamela arose.

"Sir," said she, "Captain Leach told me he would inform you that we were ready."

"So he did, madam," said I, "and I am come to help you embark."

As there was no sign of the waiting-woman's revival from her fit, I was constrained to carry her upon the deck, as I had already done from below.

The boat under command of Mr. White was already gone, for it had taken several minutes for me to bring the women upon deck. We stowed them into the long-boat, and it pushed off immediately and was lost in the smoke. We then brought up the rest of the wounded from below, who were those who had been most desperately hurt in the action. These we laid upon the deck, so as to be in readiness for lowering into the boats so soon as they should return.

In the mean time I had given orders to those not thus occupied with the wounded to load many of the guns, with slow-matches in the breeches to burn from five to ten minutes. Thus the firing might be kept up after all had left the ship, whereby we hoped that the pirates would be stayed a while from boarding and so discover our absence. In about ten minutes the gig returned without Mr. White, and the master's mate, who was in command in his stead, said that he had remained ashore with the women, as I had commanded him. In a very little while, the long-boat also returning, we got all hands aboard and pushed off, the guns still firing now and then as the slow-matches burned down. So we came safe to shore, but with no time to spare, for by the great shouts that were presently raised we knew that the pirates had come aboard the *Cassandra*, and in less than three minutes after the last man had quitted her.

Not more than fifteen or twenty minutes had been occupied in making ready and quitting the ship; for which celerity, and for the great coolness shown in this trying emergency, all praise is due both to the officers and the men. The fight had lasted for more than four hours and a half, during which time we had nine men killed, among whom was the third mate above mentioned, and twenty-two wounded, three of whom afterwards died upon the island.

Besides the clothes and valuables which many had fetched away with them* we had also brought off with us from the ship a

---

* I may say here that I myself was but poorly equipped in this respect, having not only forgot my watch, which I had left hanging in my cabin, but being also without shoes and stockings, which I had stripped off so that I might more readily swim for it if the pirates should come aboard whilst the boats were gone on their first trip to the shore. At the last moment I was so busied in supervising the lowering of the wounded into the boats that I did not think of returning for the one or of securing the other.

quantity of musquets and pistols, and a
dozen or more rounds of ammunition for
each able-bodied man. .

As soon as we landed we plunged directly into the thick brush, which there grew
close down to the edge of the beach. Having thrust our way through these thickets
for some distance, we found the others
waiting for us at a little open space at
the base of three palm - trees which stood
about two hundred yards from the shore,
it being then nigh to sunset, and with but
little chance of the pirates following us that
day.

Mr. White was standing near my passengers, who were gathered together in a group,
but one of them was missing. *It was Captain Leach.*

"And where is Captain Leach?" I cried,
looking directly at Mr. White.

He gazed at me in an exceedingly strange
manner, and I saw that he grew as pale as
death to the very lips. "And did he not

come in the boat with you, sir?" said he at last, in a low and husky voice.

At these words a terrible fear came over me. "Where is the box I gave you?" I cried; and seeing that he was not like to answer, repeated the question—"Where is the box I gave you?"

By way of reply Mr. White fumbled for a moment or two in his waistcoat-pocket, and presently handed me a scrap of paper. I opened it, and tried to read, though my hand trembled so that I could hardly contrive to make out what it was. But in spite of that, and the blurring of my eyesight, every word and every letter is stamped upon my memory as upon a plate of brass.

It was written as though in mine own handwriting, and very hastily scrawled, but so like that I could not have told it myself had I not known it to be a forgery.

These were the words:

"*Sir,—I have altered my mind in regard to the box. Please deliver it to the bearer (Captain*

Leach), *who will take present charge of it, and will convey it to me.*

                  " JOHN MACKRA."

As I still held the letter in my hand, gaz-ing stupidly at it, but seeing nothing, the whole villany of the business was, as it were, revealed to me. I saw that when Captain Leach had left the ship in the native canoe two nights ago he had come straight to the pirates and had made some bargain with them for that accursed Rose of Paradise; that when he had gone aboard the *Greenwich* and the Ostender the next day, it was not to secure a passage for himself, but rather to per-suade them to sacrifice the *Cassandra*, and so save their own wretched hulks; that when he had sent me to the women in the great cabin it was to get rid of me so that he might tamper with Mr. White; and last of all, that he had kept this forged letter about him for just such an occasion as this. Then I thought of my shipmates killed and wound-ed, of my vessel and cargo lost, of all these poor people outcasts upon this savage, desert coast, with no present prospect or hope of help, and of the stone itself thus cheated out of my hands at the last moment, and after all the suffering and the blood that had been shed. There came a great roaring in mine ears, all things began to reel ` before my sight, a dark cloud seemed to encompass me, and then I knew nothing more.

X.

AFTER I had thus swooned away, which
happened both from the fever of my wound
and the loss of blood, there followed a long
time during which everything was confused
and dream-like. I may call to mind what
seemed to me a great and toilsome journey,
but so commingled with the visions of my
fever that I knew not whether it had taken
hours, days, or weeks, and of which I may
remember almost nothing. After that I
have a memory of tossing upon a pallet
which was both rough and hard, of a dark-
ened and silent room, and of people coming
and going and talking in whispers. Then
one morning I awoke as though from a deep
sleep, and felt that the heat of the fever had
left me, though mightily weak and weary.
This awakening must have happened be-

twixt four and five o'clock in the morning, for the mat which hung at the door had been raised, and a cool and refreshing breeze swept through the mud hut.

I lay for a long time looking out of the door towards which my couch was facing, and through which I could see hillocks of gray sand intermingled with rich and luxuriant vegetation ; beyond, the rim of the ocean stretched like a black thread against the gray sky. I gave no thought to anything, but lay quite still, feeling mighty peaceful and quiet. By-and-by I turned mine eyes and saw that some one sat beside me, and that it was Mr. White. He did not see that I was observing him, but sat reading his Bible, for he was a young man of great earnestness of spirit. The sight of him brought first one thing and then another back to my memory, until the whole was complete as I have told it.

" Mr. White," said I. I spoke very quietly, but he could not have started more vio-

8

lently had a clap of thunder sounded from
· the sky. He came straight to me, and laid
his hand upon my forehead. "Yes," said I,
making shift to smile, " the fever has left me
now; and will you tell me where I am?"

"Sir," says he, " you are safe, and in the
king's town; and now I will go and tell the
surgeon of the bettering of your condition."
So saying he left me, and Mr. Greenacre,
the surgeon, presently came to me. He
told me that all hands had been brought
safe to the king's town; that I might set
my mind at rest both regarding the passengers and the crew; and that I must not now
talk further, but should seek to rest myself,
which was very necessary for me to do in
my present condition. Nor was I inclined
to disobey this command, but presently
closed mine eyes and fell into a most refreshing slumber, from which I did not
awake until nigh sunset, when I found that
Mr. White was once more beside me. When
he saw that I was awake he made as if he

would again go and call the surgeon, but I stopped him from doing as he intended.

"Stay, Mr. White," said I. "I should like now to know something more of what has happened. How long have I been lying in this condition?"

"About six days, sir," said he. And then, in a trembling voice, "Oh, Captain Mackra, can you forgive me for the injury I have done?"

"Why, sir," said I, "I have nothing to forgive, nor have you done anything for which to beseech forgiveness. What you did you did with the best intent; nor can I blame you for being so deceived by such a wicked and cunning villain as Captain Leach. And now tell me, what news is there of the pirates?" To this he answered that they were still lying at anchor in the bay on the east side of the island, repairing the damages which we had wrought; that the chief ot them was one Edward England, a fellow of great note among these wicked

villains; that they had been so enraged at
that bloody fight, which had cost them so
dear, that they had set a reward of two thousand pounds upon my head; and that the
king of the island had offered us his protection, and had undertaken to guard us securely from any attack the pirates might be
inclined to make against us. But, nevertheless, lest any of the natives should be of a
mind to betray me for this great and mag-
nificent reward, it had been deemed best
that it should be reported that I had been
killed in the late engagement.

After having recounted these things as
briefly as possible, Mr. White again went in
search of the surgeon, who soon came, and
put a very cheerful face upon my case, which
he said was now without doubt upon the
mend.

After having eaten a very hearty supper
of rich and savory broth, I was so far re-
freshed as to be able to receive some few
who particularly desired to have speech with

me, and who were presently ushered in by Mr. Greenacre.

The first to come was my former acquaintance, Mr. Longways, the Company's agent, and with him a great tall native chief, who had rather the appearance of a Malay than an African negro, and who was none other than King Kulakula himself. With these two came a black interpreter from Mozambique, for King Coffee could not speak one single word of English, but only a little Dutch, which he had picked up from the traders along the coast.

After them came the two ladies, escorted by Mr. Langely, who had now so far recovered from his wound as to be able to be about with ease, although he still carried his arm in a sling.

Mrs. Evans, when she saw me, gushed into tears, but Mistress Pamela came straight to me, took my hand, and set it to her lips, though I strove my best to stay her from doing so.

"Sir," said she, "what do we not owe to our brave preserver, who hath brought us safe through all this great trouble!"

"No, madam," cried I, hastily, for I could not bear that she should lay credit to me, who had so little earned it, seeing how helpless I had been in bringing them safe off from the *Cassandra*—"no, madam, give no credit to me; give it first of all to God, and then to Mr. Langely, who, though so sorely wounded, brought you, I understand, safe through the wilderness to this place."

After they had so spoken, comes King Kulakula forward with the interpreter, and through the black man expressed many kind and condescending wishes for the continued bettering of my condition. He furthermore gave me every assurance that we should all be protected from our enemies so long as we chose to remain at that place.

After a little while my visitors left me, except Mr. Longways, who, by permission of the surgeon, remained behind to exchange a few words with me. I then observed for the first time how sadly different he was in his appearance from what he had been; for the jauntiness of his carriage was gone, and he looked mightily perturbed in his spirits.

So soon as he had made sure that no one was by to overhear us, he began without preface to talk about the Rose of Paradise, saying that Mr. White had told him that it had been lost, and also some details of the matter; that that loss meant ruin to him, who could say no word in his own defence excepting by letter, while I had every opportunity of stating my case in my own fashion to the East India Company when I should come home, and so clear myself and leave him in the mire. But in spite of that it was his opinion that even I, with all these advantages in my favor, would have great trouble in making matters straight; for the loss of three hundred thousand pounds, besides my ship and cargo, was a thing that was not likely to be passed over very lightly.

I could hardly forbear smiling at this discourse, although it was of such a serious nature, for it seemed very strange to me that Mr. Longways should so readily suspect me of being disposed to ruin him.

" Sir," said I, " I know not what you would do in such a case as this, but I tell you plain that if I am compelled to make an unfortunate report to the East India Company, I will make it without blaming you or myself or any one, but simply tell the truth, and so let them adjudge the matter as they see fit."

" That is it, sir," cried he—" that is it, sir. If the Company are informed that I betrayed this important secret to Captain Leach, I'll have to whistle for it a long time out in the cold before I get a snug berth with them again."

" I am mightily sorry for you," said I, gravely. " But of course, sir, that is a matter concerning which you alone are responsible. Nevertheless, I must tell you that I am not inclined to leave this place without endeavoring to recover that which has been so unfortunately lost."

" What, sir !" he cried; " do you mean to say that you will undertake to recover the Rose of Paradise again ? And how do you purpose doing it, may I ask ?"

" You may ask, sir," says I, smiling; " but as for my telling you, why, that is a very different matter."

Yet I had determined upon one point almost as soon as Mr. White had informed me who was the pirate captain into whose hands the *Cassandra* had fallen, and that was to go aboard of the pirate craft, and to speak with Captain Edward England himself. I had known him before he had entered into the nefarious life which he now followed, and while he was still first mate of the *Lady Alice.* I was then with Captain Wraxel in the West Indies, and had met England at Kingston, in the island of Jamaica, upon which occasion he had appeared to conceive quite a liking for me, though I cannot say it was returned in kind. I knew him as a wild and reckless blade, but neither blood-thirsty nor cruel, and making every allowance for the change in his nature which this wicked life might effect, I did not believe that injury would happen to me if I could once gain his promise of safety in visiting his ship.

As for the jewel, I did not believe that Captain Leach would disclose the secret of it without he had been compelled to do so; wherefore, if he had it still in his own keeping, I entertained a hope that I might by some trick or other snatch the precious stone away from him again. In that event I did not believe he would say anything, for fear that the pirates might punish him for keeping it a secret from them.

But although I could perceive, as Mr. Longways had said, that it was of great importance both to his future and mine own that the Rose of Paradise should be regained, I ventured my life not so much in the hope of obtaining the stone as of procuring some means by which all hands might be able to quit the island; for we—and more especially the women—could not but be in constant danger from the bloody wretches thirsting for revenge on account of the check which we of the *Cassandra* had lately put upon them. Wherefore I thought it best that I should boldly visit the pirate captain, for I had great hopes of being able to persuade him to allow us to escape, and even of procuring from him some means to that end.

In any case, the venture could not but be of advantage to us, for even if I should perish, their revenge might thereby be satisfied, and they might depart without molesting the rest of the ship's company, for they were pleased to regard me as the chief cause of all their mishaps in the late engagement.

Before I dared venture aboard the pirate craft it was necessary that I should first write a letter to the captain, and also that I should have a trustworthy person to convey my communication to him; nor did I give two thoughts to this matter, for common justice pointed to Mr. White as the only fitting one to be my messenger; accordingly I sent for him, and he soon came. I told him that I desired to open communication with the pirate captain upon a matter of great importance, and that I gave him this opportunity towards redeeming his self-respect by conveying my message to Captain England. Nor have I ever seen a man more grateful than Mr. White upon this occasion; two or three times he strove to speak, and when he did contrive to do so it was only simply to say, " Sir, I thank you."

The surgeon having given me permission, I wrote my letter, and Mr. White took it that very night, having no companion with him but two natives who acted as guides. I have a copy of the letter, made at the time, which runs as follows:

" *To Captain Edward England :*

" *Sir,—I write you this in a most forlorn and distressing situation.*

" *Having defended ourselves, our ship, and those intrusted to our keeping, from you, who sought to encompass our destruction by all means in your power, we now find ourselves reduced to the necessity of imploring aid from you, who so lately sought our lives. Nor would we even yet ask anything from you were it not for three poor and helpless women, whose safety here is a matter of uncertainty from day to day, and who, without aid is extended to them, may perish miserably in this desolate and savage land.*

" *Sir, though a wild and ungoverned nature, I never knew you to be a cruel man; therefore I ask this aid of you for the sake of these three women.*

" *Furthermore, I ask that you do not hastily refuse this plea for aid, but may allow me to come aboard of your craft and speak to you in person.*

" *I know that there is with you one who is mine enemy, because of a great injury which he hath done me, and who will no doubt conspire against my life—I mean Captain Leach, lately one of my passengers, and who, I suspect, along with others, betrayed us into your hands. But although I be-*

lieve he would seek my life, yet I am willing to trust it into your hands if you will promise me safety in my coming and my going.

" Sir, I beseech you to grant me this speech with you, that I may plead the cause of the weak and helpless, and am, sir,

" Your very obedient and humble servant,

" JOHN MACKRA.*"*

XI.

MR. WHITE was only gone for a little more than two days, and when he returned he brought with him a letter from the pirate captain. The communication ran thus:

"*To Captain John Mackra, late of the 'Cassandra:'*

"*Sir,—If you choose to risk your life by coming hither, devil a word have I to say against it. They're a wild set of blades under me, and mind the helm no better than a washing-tub, so that my orders have little or no weight with them. All the same, if you're the man to come aboard, and have the courage to face the matter out, I'll do what I can to see that no harm happens to you. But if you'll take a friend's advice you'll stay where you are, and let a bad matter cure itself, for you know very well that there is no use splicing a rotten rope. As for the pickle you're in, lay that to your luck, and not to me.*

"EDWARD ENGLAND."

I was none too well pleased with this precious epistle, for I could see very readily how little command Captain England held upon the wretches under him. Nevertheless, it did not alter my determination to to go aboard of the pirate craft and to speak with him. I was the more inclined to do this as I felt well assured that the pirates could not now be as hot for my blood as they had been at first.

It was necessary for me to get away from the king's town without confiding my determination to any one, or any one having knowledge of my departure, for I knew very well that there was not one of my officers but would have stayed me from acting on my plans had they been informed of them, even if they should find it needful to use force to prevent my going.

It was the evening of the eighth day since the fight when Mr. White returned with Captain England's letter, and I determined that that very night should witness my departure upon my enterprise, which to one looking coolly upon it might seem little if any better than the frantic act of a madman. Nor was it that I myself was unconscious of the magnitude of these dangers, for I entered upon them only because that in the desperate state of our necessities I could see no other course out of our difficulties, and so had to choose this for lack of a better. Accordingly, as said above, I determined to set out that very night, for nothing could be gained by further delay.

There was no other choice left me but to make my way along the beach, which, although it would increase the distance by five or six miles, would yet afford me a sound and level highway for my journeying, the sand being firm and hard when the water was out at low tide.

That night I wrote a lengthy letter to Mr. Langely, giving him full particulars as to what I was about to undertake, and also

9

instructions as to how he should proceed in the event of my not returning from my adventure. I also wrote my will, and settled all my affairs as well as I was able. This took until nigh midnight.

All this I managed to do without the knowledge of any one, and by the light of a little wick floating in a dish of oil, the flame of which I kept so well shaded that no one perceived it in all that time.

About one o'clock I came out from my hut, and found the stars shining most beautifully in the sky, and all the air full of the noises of the night. I did not tarry, however, but walked straight to the beach, and along it towards the northern end of the island, around which and beyond the cape I knew the bay to lie, about ten leagues distant from the king's town.

I had only been twice upon my feet since the fever had left me, and found that I was far more weak than I had supposed myself to be, so that I had to rest myself at frequent intervals. However, I managed to cover some ten miles of my journey by about six o'clock in the morning, by which time I was so exhausted that I could go no farther, but had to lie down under the shade of the bushes and rest myself for a long time.

I speak of these things to show why it was that my journey should have occupied nigh upon two days, for it was not until the afternoon of the second day that I came within sight of a boat, drawn up on the beach, which I knew to belong to the pirates, and from which the crew had gone into the thickets, either to search for game or for water.

I had eaten nothing all that day, for I had not thought that my journey would have taken me so long, and I did not care to burden myself with any more food than necessary. So I was glad to see the boat, not only being very weary, but also having my feet so badly blistered by the unwonted exposure to the hot sun on the bare sand that it was only with pain that I could take a single step.

As I drew nigh, two fellows who had been lying in the shade upon the further side sprang to their feet and hailed me.

"Who are you?" says one of them—a great black-bearded fellow with a dirty yellow handkerchief tied around his head, a ragged scarf about his loins, a brace of pistols hanging from a leathern belt, and a dirty shirt opened at the breast, showing a hairy throat and chest.

"I am Captain John Mackra," said I, and I sat down upon the gunwale of the boat, for I could go no farther.

"The devil you are!" says he, and he stared at me from top to toe as though I had been some strange creature the like of which he had never beheld before. Then, without another word, he put his fingers to his lips and gave a great, long, shrill whistle. I presently heard a great crackling in the

"I AM CAPTAIN JOHN MACKRA," SAID I, AND I SAT DOWN UPON THE GUNWALE OF THE BOAT.

bushes and the noise of loud voices, and soon there burst out of the thickets six or eight great, bearded, dirty, villanous rascals, who came running down to the boat, having caught sight of me, and knowing me to be a stranger. "It's Captain Leach," said the one of the pirates who had not yet spoken —a young fellow of not more than twenty.

Some of those who had just come had been drinking, as could be very plainly seen from the way in which they acted. One of them was for killing me off-hand, and I verily believe would have done so, in spite of all that the others could do or say, had not another of them knocked him down with an oar with such a blow that I thought at first the fellow had been killed outright.

After that they bound me hand and foot, and chucked me into the stern-sheets of the boat along with the fellow who had been knocked down by the oar, and who lay without life or motion, as though neither were of more account than so much old junk.

After that they shoved off from the beach in the direction of my old craft the *Cassandra*, which rode at anchor about a mile and a half or two miles away.

The boat had hardly come alongside when the news of my coming ran fore and aft like a train of powder. They hoisted me upon deck and laid me just aft of the main-mast, whilst a great crowd gathered round me and stared at me, some of them grinning and some of them cursing me.

Most of them were more or less in liquor, and it was this circumstance that came nigh to costing me my life, and this was how it happened:

One great fellow with a dreadful scar across his face gave me a kick in the loins which I thought at first had finished me, and for no cause that I could see but that he was drunk and in a savage humor. One or two of them sang out to him not to kill me just then, but he made no answer except by aiming another kick at my head, which

I warded off with my arm so that it did me little or no harm. He drew back his foot for another blow, but just then an iron belaying-pin came whizzing through the air and struck the fellow in the jaw, knocking him down upon the deck as though he had been shot.

I turned mine eyes and saw that it was Captain England himself who had struck the blow.

"Look 'ee," says he, "we'll have none of this; if killing is to be done, it is to be done lawyer-like. He's come aboard himself, and if he's to be killed he's to be killed after his trial, and not before."

There was a moment or two of pause, for Captain England had drawn a brace of pistols, and held one cocked in either hand; but just then up stepped a fellow who it was very plain to see was of some account amongst them, for his clothes were of rich stuff, and he had a gold chain with a cross slung around his neck, and golden ear-rings in his ears.   He walked up to England until he stood face to face with him.

"Look 'ee, Ned England," says he, "what I've got to say is this: you're carrying things with too high a hand to suit us easy-going fellows.   D'ye think you're king or emperor, and that we're nigger slaves, that you knock us about as it suits your humor?"

I had expected that England would have shot the fellow down where he stood, but he stayed his hand, and by the muttering of the rest I knew that the speaker carried most of them with him.

"Look 'ee, now," says he, more boldly, "didn't we choose you for our captain ourselves?   And here you knock us around with belaying-pins as though you owned every man of us; and all for what?   Why, for giving this here precious sea-captain an innocent kick or two for all of the good fellows he's sent to h—ll since ten days ago. What I say is, hang him up to the yard-arm;" and he fetched me a terrible kick in the side without taking his eyes from his captain's face.

At this time, although I heard what was said, I thought but little of what was passing about me, my mind being beclouded with my weakness and my pains, for I had wellnigh swooned from the agony of those two kicks upon my flank and loins. Therefore I lay with mine eyes shut, feeling deathly sick and faint.

A time of silence followed, though how long it might be I could not exactly tell. Then I heard Captain England speak, the words coming to my ears as though from a great distance, because of my condition.

" D—n you, Burke, what do I care for the fellow? If you want the man's life, take it!" and I knew that he swung upon his heel and walked away.

XII.

I COULD not at that minute see that any-thing stood between me and death, for the pirates were so bent upon my immediate destruction that they set about getting ready a line to hang me up without more ado.

Yet though I had cause to apprehend that the very next moment would be my last upon earth, the dread of death was in no wise keen upon me, for in my half-swoon I lay as one in a dream, and neither saw nor heard very clearly the preparations they were making for my destruction, and so was mercifully spared that pain. But God in His great mercy determined it otherwise than was the intention of these wicked men, for just at that moment some one forward began bawling out, in a great hoarse voice, " Where is Jack Mackra? Where is he, I

say? Show him to me! —— —— ——
ye! out of my way, and let me get at him!"

As I might turn my head, I looked
whence my voice came, and there saw, as in
a dream, a great, tall, lantern-jawed man,
with a patch over one eye and a crutch under his left arm. In his right hand he held
a long sharp knife, with which he jabbed at
those who stood in his way, so that they
were glad enough to make room for him,
one or two of them cursing him, the others
grinning and laughing as though it were all
a fine piece of sport. As those around me
drew aside I beheld him more plainly; his
left leg had been cut off at the knee, he was
loose-jointed and ungainly, and he had one
of the most villanous countenances that it
was ever my fortune to look into. I could
also see that he, like many of the others,
had been drinking. It was very plain that
he was a great favorite amongst the rest, for
they made room for him and took all his
curses and many blows, which he gave with

his crutch, without either answering him or striving to defend themselves. Even the fellow who had spoken so boldly to the captain's face, and whom I afterwards found to be the chief of the "lords," as they are pleased to call those in authority amongst them, grinned and stood aside as the villanous cripple came and leaned over me.

"D—n you," says he, "and is it you, Jack Mackra? Then I have a score to pay you that has stood on the slate for this many a day."

He turned me over upon my face with his crutch, and the next moment I felt the cords that tied my hands give way, and knew that they had been cut, then my legs and feet were loosened from their lashings, and I was a free man. I heard the fellow say, "Get up!" whereupon I stood upon my feet and gazed about me, though my brain still swam, and all things appeared blurred and distorted to my sight, the sky and the sea and the faces around me being all strangely mingled together. Then presently, as my confusion began to fade away from me, I heard the one-legged man speaking to me.

"And do you know who I am?" said he.

" No," says I, at last gathering my wits to speak; " I cannot bring you to mind."

" Why," says he, "don't you remember Jimmy Ward, the cook aboard the *Pembroke Castle*—him as you saved from five drunken Spanish devils over at Honduras? Hey? don't you mind how they had me down under the table, jabbing at me with their d—d snickershees and swearing that they would cut the living heart out of me? If it hadn't been for you, it would have been all over with Jimmy Ward at that time." He waited for an answer, but as yet I could say nothing. " Well, I haven't forgot it if you have," he continued; " I owe you a good turn, and I'll pay it if I have to bleed for it."

Just then up steps the fellow who had

faced England so boldly a moment or two before. "Come, come, Jimmy," says he, "a joke's a joke, and I can laugh as loud as any; but here's a man has done us more damage than anybody we've fell in with since we ran foul of the *Eagle*."

"Hang him up!" Hang him up!" sang out several of those who stood around, and I verily believe the business would have gone against me, after all, only for Captain England, who must have been near for all this time, and who came to the aid of the cripple. Both together, they contrived so to argue and talk and threaten the others that the end of the matter was they led me off to the captain's cabin, the one on one side of me and the other on the other, whilst the crowd followed behind, though they came no further than the door, which was clapped to in their faces.

"You've had a narrow miss of it," says England, so soon as we were come fairly within and had sat down, "and you've nobody to thank for it but yourself, for if you'd minded what I told you you'd have staid where you were and let your bad luck sail her own craft without putting your hand to the helm. Even yet I don't know if we'll be able to get you off, for Tom Burke is hot for your blood, and will get it if he's able."

" That he will," says Ward ; " for he's not the man to give up what he's laid his hand to."

" Have you had anything to eat ?" said England, presently.

" Not since five o'clock this morning," said I.

" Why," said he, " you'll have to be fed, whether they hang you or no." Whereupon he fetched out from a locker a great lot of biscuit and a decanter of the very port-wine with which I had entertained Mr. Long-ways when he came aboard the *Cassandra* with The Rose of Paradise ; nor have I ever tasted food that was more refreshing than that which I then ate, for I was wellnigh exhausted with hunger.

No one spoke for a while, and England walked up and down the cabin with his hands clasped behind his back. During all this time I had been looking around me, and of a sudden my heart seemed to leap into my throat, for in the corner of the cabin, lying amongst a lot of litter, where it seemed to have been flung as of no account, I saw the iron despatch-box.

My danger had been so great and my mind in such a maze for all this time that there had been no room in my brain for other matters, the very objects of my adventure having been forgotten for a while; but with the sight of this everything came back to me with a rush, and I wondered for the first time that I had not yet seen my betrayer.

"Where is Captain Leach?" said I to England.

He stopped short in his walk, and regarded me with a very strange expression, which at the time I could in no wise understand.

"Why," says he, presently, "he was shot —shot by accident — when we first came aboard of this here craft after you left her."

I sat silent for a great long time after this, nor could I think of one word to say, for of all the things which my mind had forecasted, this was the very furthest from my imaginings. So I sat staring at the pirate captain, who, upon his part, sat gazing back again at me, answering my look with a grin. I had been well assured that Captain Leach had stolen the jewel, but was it possible that I had misjudged him in suspecting that he had betrayed us to the pirates, and that they, finding him alive upon the vessel, whence he had not had sufficient time to escape, had thereupon instantly murthered him, as is their custom upon such occasions?

10

" And tell me this," said I at last, "was it through Captain Leach's machinations that we were betrayed into your hands ?"

" Why," says he, " I may tell you plain, if I had never met Captain Leach I should never have ventured into this harbor in the face of three armed vessels lying across the channel."

" Then I was not mistaken," said I. But I dared ask no more questions, lest the pirate captain's suspicions should be aroused, for, from the appearance of the despatch-box, which did not yet seem to have been tampered with, but rather held as of no account whatever, I did not believe that Captain Leach had betrayed the presence of the jewel to the pirate, but rather had reserved the secret for his own advantage, which, indeed, was the most likely supposition that could be imagined. If now I could but by some means or other contrive to find opportunity to examine the box, I could very speedily tell whether the lock had been forced; which would, in my estimation, decide whether or not the jewel was still safe and undiscovered.

Presently Ward spoke. " And how," said he, "did you come to get into such a pickle as I found you, sir?"

I told him the main reason for my visit in as few words and with as little circumlocution as possible; how I had entertained hopes of procuring a promise of safety for my passengers and ship's crew, and even possibly of obtaining some means of transportation from the place where they now were to one of greater ease and security. Both men listened without a word to what I said, and when I had ended Ward pursed his mouth up in a most comical fashion, and gave a great long whistle, half under his breath, regarding me the while with his one eye as round as a saucer.

" And do you mean to say," says he, " that you, a sick man, have gone and travelled ten leagues all for to give yourself up to such a gang of bloody cutthroats as we be?"

"Why, yes," says I; "sure ten leagues is not such a long journey that one need make much of a stir about it."

"Ten leagues be blowed!" says he. "Suppose they had shot you dead when they had found out who you were; what then?"

"But they did not shoot me," said I.

"But perhaps they may kill you yet," put in England.

"That matter is neither in your hands nor mine," said I.

Ward looked in a very droll manner, first at England and then at me. "Well, I'm blowed!" he said at last.

At this Captain England burst into a great loud laugh. "Why," says he, "it would be a vast pity to let a man of such spirit lose his life after all. What d'ye say, Ward?"

"I say yes," said Ward, and he thumped his fist down on the table; "and by the

Eternal he shall get what he wants—in reason—Tom Burke and the devil notwithstanding!"

"Come," says England; "come, Ward, we'll go and fetch Burke in, and see if we can't drink him into a good humor." And so saying both men went out of the cabin, shutting the door behind them. As soon as their backs were turned I sprang to where the despatch-box lay, snatched it up, and began eagerly examining it. It was still securely locked; the lid had not been forced, and I could see no marks of violence upon it. But I had just then but short time for such an examination, for in a little while I heard footsteps outside, whereupon I replaced the box where I had found it and resumed my chair, composing my countenance as far as I was able to do. Presently I heard voices at the door, and from their tones I could gather that Captain England and the crippled cook were trying to persuade Burke to come into the cabin, he being mightily unwilling to do so. For a while they held the door ajar, and I could hear Burke cursing and swearing at a great rate, and calling Heaven to witness that he would have my life before he was done with me. Meantime the others were busied in talking to him, and soothing him, and reasoning with him, but all to no purpose. No; he would come in and drink a glass of grog with them, if that was what they were after, but he would have my life — yes, he would; and he was not to be wheedled out of his purpose by soft words either. So they, after a while, all came into the cabin and sat down to the table, though Burke never so much as turned his eyes in my direction.

Captain England brought out a bottle of Jamaica, which he set upon the board, and each of the three pirates mixed himself a glass of grog. Burke drank three or four glasses of the stuff without its seeming in the least to smooth his ill-temper. The cripple kept pace with him in his drinking, at which I was mightily anxious, for when such bloody wretches as they become heated with liquor, it is a toss of a farthing whether they murder a man in their sport or lavish caresses upon him. However, I was glad to see that Captain England drank but sparingly, wherefore I entertained great hopes that he would remain sufficiently cool to prevent any violence being used against me.

But I greatly doubt that my life would have been in danger under any circumstances, for after a while, as Burke became more warmed in his cups, his displeasure against me became more and more softened. At first, without speaking directly to me, he began, with many imprecations upon his own head, to say that though he was a bloody sea-pirate, and a murderer, and a thief, he knew a man of courage when he saw him, and loved him as his brother. By-and-by he insisted upon shaking hands with

me across the table, swearing that if harm
had happened to me through him he would
have repented it to the very last day of his
life. I now perceived that the time had
come for me to act; accordingly I began,
first by hints and afterwards by direct ap-
peals, to beseech them that they would give
me the smaller of their two crafts, which
had been so injured in the late engagement
that it was still lying upon the beach where
they had run it aground, and from which
position they had made no efforts to rescue
it. I had noticed the craft as I came down
the beach, and though I observed that she
had been very much shattered by the broad-
sides which we had fired into her, I yet had
hopes that if I could get possession of her
I might be able to patch her up sufficiently to transport my passengers and crew to
some place of greater security than the isl-
and offered, even perhaps to Bombay, weather permitting. I had thought that the pirates would have made some objection, and I

believe that even England himself was star-
tled at the boldness of my request, for he
looked anxiously at the others, but ventured
nothing. However, I think that that very
boldness recommended itself to these reckless spirits, for they granted what I desired
with hardly a word of objection. Embold-
ened by this, I went still further, and be-
sought them to give me back some of the
cargo which they had captured along with
the *Cassandra.*

At this, though he said nothing, Captain
England grinned as though vastly amused.
Nor was I wrong in venturing such a seem-
ingly foolhardy request, for not only did
they promise to give me back one hundred
and twenty - nine bales of the Company's
goods, but also gave me a written agreement to that effect, which they each of them
signed, Captain England first of all.

I may say here that though it might seem
absurd to set any value upon a mere written agreement signed by such bloody and

lawless men, it was really of very great moment, for these fellows have a vast respect
and regard for any instrument to which
they set their hand, wherefore I knew that
the chances were many to one that they
would do as they promised, after once having superscribed to it.

Then, with my heart beating so that I
could hardly speak, I turned to Captain
England. "And you, sir," said I, "will you
grant me one small favor?"

"That depends upon what it is," says he.

I looked at him steadily for a moment or
two whilst I was collecting myself; then I
spoke with all the coolness I could command, although I felt that I could scarcely
forbear trembling at this trying moment.
"Why, sir," says I, "if my despatches are
lost, I can make but a poor sort of a report
to the Honorable Company."

"Well, John Mackra, and how can I help
you in that?" said he, very coolly.

"Easily enough," said I. "Yonder is my

despatch-box in the corner, which can be of but little use to you, and yet it is of great import to me."

"And you want it?" says he.

"Indeed yes," said I, "though of course that is as you please."

He regarded me for a while in silence, his head upon one side, and his face twisted up into a most droll, quizzical, cunning expression, of which I could make nothing whatever.

"And is that all that you want of me?" said he.

I nodded my head, for I could not trust myself to speak.

Upon this he burst suddenly into a great loud laugh, and gave the table a thump with his fist which made the glasses jingle. I sat regarding him, not knowing what to make of it all; but his next words were a vast relief to me.

"Why," says he, "I thought you were going to ask me for something of some account. If that is all you want, it is yours, and welcome to it."

Finding all three of the pirates to be in such a complacent mood, I asked them for some of my clothes, for those that I had hung in tatters about me, and, as said before, I was in my bare feet. But this they would not do, Master Burke asking me whether they had not granted enough already, without giving me togs to cover my bloody carcass. Upon this I perceived that I had gotten all that I was likely to obtain, and so had to go without my clothes.

The pirates were for keeping me on board all night, that they might, as they were pleased to say, entertain me in a decent fashion. But I, having gained possession of the precious despatch-box, and trembling with anxiety lest by some sudden shift of luck it should be taken away from me again, was most eagerly anxious to take myself away. England himself urged my departure. So about seven o'clock I was put

ashore, with the despatch-box in my possession, giving thanks that I had come off from
my adventure with such exceeding good
fortune, for I felt that I had not only recovered the most precious prize of all, but
England had promised to do his uttermost
to hold the others to their written agreement, saying that if he were successful he
would depart in two days, leaving the bales
of goods behind upon the shore.

XIII.

ENGLAND himself chose a crew to row me across the beach, and I have no doubt selected the least reprehensible of all the gang; for although they said little to me, they showed no disposition either to be insolent or to offer violence to me; one of them even took off his jacket and laid it in the stern-sheets for me to sit upon. And truly, in spite of their wicked ways, there is not so much difference betwixt some of these fellows and the common sailors in our merchant service, excepting that the poor wretches have been led astray by evil counsel until they have broken the laws and committed outrages upon the high-seas, and so are become outlawed and desperate. Moreover, I believe there are many of them who would return to better ways had they opportunity of so doing, and were not afraid of suffering for the evil things which they have committed.

But at that time I thought little or nothing of how they regarded me, my only desire being to get ashore, that I might hide the precious despatch-box in some place of safety. This I did as soon as might be after I had landed, burying the casket in the sand, and marking the place so that I might know it again.

Some little distance beyond where I had been put ashore from the pirate boat I came upon a party of my own men under Mr. White, who had been despatched after me by Mr. Langely so soon as he had read the communication which I had left behind me at the king's town, and who had for some time been lying hidden in the thickets, whence they might observe the pirates and still remain unseen by them.

I may confess that I was mightily glad to behold such kind and friendly faces again, nor did they seem less rejoiced than myself at the meeting. They would not allow me to walk, but making a litter of two saplings, bore me by turns upon the way, so that against the morning had come we were safe in the king's town once more.

Mr. Longways was among the first to visit me, and betrayed the most lively signs of joy upon finding that I had been fortunate enough to secure the great ruby once more, though he regretted that I had not fetched the box with me instead of having buried it in the sand, so that we might have assured ourselves of the safety of the treasure. Upon this point I put him at his ease by convincing him that the box was in such a condition and of such an appearance as to make me feel certain that it had neither been forced nor the lock tampered with.

We only remained in the king's town about three days longer; at the end of that time the lookout which we had placed at the cape came in and reported that the pirate crafts had hoisted sail and borne away to the southward, leaving behind them the battered hulk of the smallest vessel, as they had promised to do. This much many had expected of them, but I doubt if any excepting myself had ventured to hope that they would fulfil the other part of the agreement to which they had superscribed, viz., to leave behind them the bales of goods which in their half-drunken fit of generosity they had promised. Yet there they were, neatly stacked upon the beach, and even covered with a tarpaulin. And I know not whether it may be merely superstition upon their part or no, but this much I have frequently observed, that sailors of whatever condition have such a vast regard and respect for any paper or written document that they will go to great extremity before they will do aught to rupture or disobey the articles of such a bond. So it was that I was not so much surprised at this fulfilment as either Mr. Langely or Mr. White.

11

By this time I was sufficiently recovered of my fever and of my wound to take upon me the direction of affairs once more; accordingly, in the space of two weeks, we had so far patched up the battered hulk of the pirate craft as to make her tolerably sea - worthy, provided we encountered no great stress of weather.

It took us about a week longer to victual and water the vessel (the bales of goods which I had begged from the pirates having been already stowed away under cover), so that it was not until the 18th of August that we were able to leave the country— which we did, giving thanks for all the mercies that had been vouchsafed to us in this trying and terrible time.

We were becalmed off the coast of Arabia, where we suffered greatly from the scarcity of water; but being brought safely through that and other dangers, we arrived at last at Bombay, where we dropped anchor early in the afternoon of the 13th of October, it being nigh upon two months since we had left the coast of Juanna.

I immediately sent a message to the Governor, Mr. Boon, notifying him of the safe arrival of Mistress Pamela, and that I was now ready to deliver the despatch - box at such time as he should choose to appoint. I also forwarded to him by the messenger a full report of all that had happened, and of the loss of the *Cassandra* in the engagement on the 23d of July.

In about an hour and a half Mr. Boon came aboard. He spoke most kindly and flatteringly of the service which he was pleased to say I had rendered the Company. He urged me to accompany him to the shore, but though I was mightily inclined to accept of his kindness, I was forced to decline at that time; for, finding that the Company's ship, the *City of London*, was about ready to sail, I had determined to send by her a brief account of the things herein narrated, and was at that moment engaged in writing the letter which was afterwards so widely published both in the newspapers and in Captain Johnson's book relating to the lives of the nine famous pirate captains. Finding that I could not just then quit the ship, he insisted that I should sup with them that very night. I was only too glad to accept of this, for I had determined that I would discover in what manner of regard Mistress Pamela held me, and that without loss of time. I had now every right to offer my addresses to her, which I had not had heretofore. Accordingly, having delivered the despatch - box into Mr. Boon's hands with feelings of the most sincere and heart-felt relief, and having obtained his receipt for the same, I escorted Mistress Pamela to the Governor's boat, thence returning to my own cabin feeling strangely lonely and melancholic.

This was about half-past two o'clock in the afternoon; at about four a small boat came alongside, and a young man of some twenty-three years of age stepped upon the deck, who introduced himself as Mr. Whitcomb, the Governor's secretary. He brought a written message from the Governor, requesting my immediate presence at the Residency upon a matter of the very first importance. I turned to Mr. Whitcomb and asked if he knew what was the nature of the business the Governor would have with me.

He said no, but that the Governor and Mr. Elliott, the Company's agent, had been closeted together with Mr. McFarland and Mr. Hansel, of the banking-house, for some time, and then had sent this message to me by him, which was plainly one of very great consequence.

I immediately entered the boat with the secretary, and was rowed to the shore, where, when we had come to the Residency, I found the four gentlemen waiting for me. They were seated around a table, whereon was the despatch-box and my written report, which consumed some six or eight sheets of paper.

The Governor invited me to be seated, which I had hardly done when one of the company, whom I afterwards found to be Mr. Elliott, began questioning me. I answered fully to everything he asked, the others listening, and now and then putting in a word, or asking for fuller particulars upon some point or other which was perhaps more obscure. When I came to the part that related to Captain Leach I saw them glance at one another in a very peculiar way; but I continued without stopping until I had told everything concerning the matter from the beginning to the end. No one said anything for a little time, until at last Mr. Elliott spoke:

" Do I correctly understand from this report," says he, touching the papers which lay upon the table as he spoke, " that Mr. Longways betrayed the nature of the contents of the despatch-box both to you and to Captain Leach?"

" Yes, sir," said I.

"And you are sure that no one knew of the presence of the jewel but you and he?"

"Yes, sir," said I, again.

At this the gentlemen exchanged glances, and Mr. Elliott continued his questioning.

"And did you not know that Captain Leach had been left behind when you quitted the *Cassandra?*"

"Why, no, sir," said I. "It was intended that he should go in the first passage of the long-boat with the boatswain."

"But did you not say that you helped the women aboard of the long-boat?"

"Yes, sir, I did," I said.

There was a pause of a moment or two, and all sat regarding me. Presently Mr. Elliott spoke again.

"And did you not then see that Captain Leach was absent from the boat?" said he.

"No, sir," said I, "I did not; the boat was very full, and the air so thick with gunpowder smoke that I could see little or nothing at any distance."

" But did you not then take care to see that all your passengers were safe aboard ?"

" Why, no, sir," said I. " The order had been passed for all passengers to go aboard the long-boat, and I supposed that Captain Leach had obeyed with the rest. I was so occupied with the safety of the women just then that I thought of nothing else."

" You say that the pirate England told you that Captain Leach had been killed when they first came aboard the *Cassandra.* Did you take any other evidence in the matter than his word ?"

" Why, no, sir," said I, " I did not."

Mr. Elliott said " Humph !" and another short space of silence followed, during which he played absently with the leaves of my report.

" But tell me, Captain Mackra," said he, presently, " did you not speak to any one of your suspicions concerning Captain Leach

after he had quitted the ship on the night
of the 21st in such a mysterious manner ?"

" Why, no, sir," said I; "for I saw no sufficient grounds to accuse him of any under-
hand practices."

"And yet," said a thin, middle-aged gentleman, with a sharp voice, whom I afterwards found to be Mr. McFarland—"and
yet you saw him quit the *Cassandra* in a
most suspicious manner, and under the most
suspicious circumstances, and also had reason to suspect him of having knowledge of
the jewel.   Why, then, did you not examine
him publicly or put him under arrest after
he returned ?"

" Sir," said I, " I disliked Captain Leach,
and feared that my prejudice might lead me
astray."

" But, Captain Mackra," said the Govern-
or, " your personal feelings should never in-
terfere with your duty."

I knew not where all these matters tended, but I began to be mightily troubled in my mind concerning them. However, I had little time for thought, for Mr. Elliott began questioning me again. He asked me if I had told any one of my intended visit to the pirate-ship, of whom I had seen there, and of what inducements I had offered to persuade them to give me one of their crafts and return such a quantity of the Company's goods. He cross-questioned me so keenly in regard to the last point that I found myself tripping more than once, for it is mightily difficult to remember all of the petty details even of such an important event as that. I believe that I answered more loosely than I otherwise would have done from the agitation into which I was cast by the serious shape which matters seemed to be taking.

" Sir," I cried to Mr. Elliott, "do you blame me for getting back so much of the Company's goods as I was able ?"

" I blame you for nothing, Captain Mackra," said he. " I merely question you in regard to a matter of great importance."

" But, sir," I said, hotly, "am I to be blamed for losing my ship after a hard-fought battle? You should recollect, sir, that I was wounded in the Company's service; methinks, sir, that should weigh some in my favor."

" But, Captain Mackra," said Mr. McFarland, very seriously, "are not accidents likely to happen to any one under any circumstances? Captain Leach, you may remember, was killed in spite of all the precautions he may have taken to preserve his life."

A great weight of dread seemed to have been settling upon me as the examination had progressed, but at these words it was as though a sudden light flashed upon me; I rose slowly from my chair, and stood with my hand leaning upon the table. For a moment or two my head swam with vertigo, and I passed my hand across my forehead.

" I am not so well, gentlemen," said I, "as I was some time since, for I have gone through many hardships; therefore I beseech you to excuse me if I have appeared weak in the manner or the matter of my discourse." Then turning to the Governor, "Will you be pleased to tell me, sir, what all this means?"

" Sir," said he, in a low tone, "the ruby has been stolen, and was not in the box when you gave it to me."

I stood looking around at them for a while; I know that I must have been very pale, for Mr. McFarland sprang to his feet.

" Captain Mackra, you are ill," he said; " will you not be seated?"

I shook my head impatiently, and collecting myself, I said, very slowly and somewhat unsteadily, " Do you suspect me of being instrumental in taking it?"

No one answered for an instant. Then the Governor said, " No, Captain Mackra, we suspect you of nothing; only it is best

I ROSE SLOWLY FROM MY CHAIR, AND STOOD WITH MY HAND LEANING UPON THE TABLE.

that you should return to England and make your report to the Company in person. Meanwhile you will make no effort to leave this country until I find means to secure your passage for you."

" I am to consider myself under arrest?" said I.

" No, sir," said the Governor, kindly, " not under arrest; but you must hold yourself prepared to stand your examination before the proper agents of the Company at London, and at such time as they may decide upon."

XIV.

So soon as I had left the Residency I went straight aboard my craft. I entered my cabin, locked the door, and began pacing up and down, striving to collect my thoughts and to shape them into some sort of order. At first I was possessed with a most ungovernable fury—that I, who had suffered so much, who had fought till I could fight no more, and who had freely risked my life in the Company's cause, should now be accused of stealing that very thing that had cost me such suffering and so great a weight of trouble. But by-and-by the ferment of my spirits began somewhat to subside, and I could look matters more coolly in the face. Then, instead of anger, I became consumed with anxiety, for I began, little by little, to perceive what a dreadful cloud of suspicion overshadowed me. I had acted to the best of my light in not accusing Captain Leach of what I feared might be unfounded suspicions bred of my dislike of his person. Now all men would think that I was leagued with him in robbing the Company of the great ruby. In return for my forbearance in not making a public accusation against him, he had betrayed me and all that were aboard the *Cassandra*, and now every one would believe that I had aided him in that as in the rest. He had remained behind in the hopes of joining the pirates, and so securing himself in the possession of his booty. Instead of accomplishing this, he had perished miserably on board of that craft, wet with the blood of those whom he had betrayed; but as for me, how could I ever disprove the horrid charge that I had deserted my confederate in guilt, leaving him to his death, so that I might gain all for myself. The very fact of my taking my life into my hands, and going so freely among those wicked and bloody wretches, instead of weighing in my favor, would seem to point to some sort of bargain with them whereby I was the gainer; for who would believe that they would voluntarily have resigned so great a part of those things which they had a short time before torn away from us at the cost of so much blood? Even the fact of my having so carefully guarded the secret of the stone might be twisted into sinister suspicions against me.

As for those bright hopes that I had but lately entertained, how could I now raise my eyes towards Mistress Pamela, or how could I look for anything, who was stained with such dreadful suspicions, without prospect of being cleansed from them?

Perceiving all these things so clearly, I resigned myself to the depths of gloomy despair, for the more I bent my mind upon these matters the less did I see my way clear from my entanglements. I sat long

into the night, thinking and thinking, until
the temptation came upon me to shoot out
my brains, and be quit of all my troubles in
that sudden manner. In this extremity I
flung myself upon my knees and prayed
most fervently, and after a while was more
at peace, though with no clearer knowledge
as to how I might better my condition. So
I went to my berth, where I was presently
sound asleep, with all my troubles forgot.

A day or two after these things had befallen comes one of the Company's clerks
aboard, with an order from Mr. Elliott relieving me of my command, and appointing
Mr. Langely in my stead. This appoint-
ment Mr. Langely would have refused had
I not urged him to accept of it, seeing he
could better settle the affairs of which he
would be in charge than one who would
come aboard a stranger. Accordingly he
consented to do as I advised, though pro-
testing against it most earnestly.

About two weeks after our arrival at Bom-

12

bay the Governor notified me that the Company's ship *Lavinia* was about quitting her anchorage, and that he had secured a berth to England in her for me. I was very well pleased that the Governor had hit upon this one ship of all others in the Company's service, for her commander, Captain Croker, was an old and well-tried friend of mine, and one with whom it would be more pleasing to be consociated at a time of such extreme ill fortune as I was then suffering under. I went aboard her at once, and was most kindly received by Captain Croker, whom I found had had a very comfortable berth fitted up for me, and had arranged all things to make my voyage as pleasant as possible.

The day after I came aboard, wind and tide being fair, and Captain Croker having received his orders, we hoisted anchor and sailed out of the harbor, and by four o'clock had dropped the land astern.

During the first part of that voyage, before I had contrived to leave the *Lavinia*, of which I shall hereafter tell, my mind was constantly and continually filled with my troubles, so that they were the first thing which I remembered in the morning, and the last thing which I forgot before I fell asleep. But that which puzzled me more than anything else was to account for the mysterious manner in which the Rose of Paradise had been spirited away from the iron despatch-box, and what had become of it after it had passed from Mr. White's possession. Of this I thought and pondered until my brain grew weary.

One night, we being at that time becalmed off the Gulf of Arabia, I sat upon the poop-deck looking out over the water and into the sky, dusted all over with an infinite quantity of stars, and with my mind still moving upon the same old track which it had so often travelled before. I know not whether it was the refreshing silence which reigned all about me, but of a sudden it

seemed as though the uncertainties which
had beset my mind were removed, and the
whole matter stood before me with a most
marvellous clearness. Then I knew, as
plain as though it had been revealed to me,
that the only man in the world who either
had the Rose of Paradise in his possession,
or knew where it was hidden, was Captain
Edward England.

I do not think that I came to this con-
clusion through any line of reasoning, but
rather with a sudden leap of thought; but
as soon as I had fairly grasped it I mar-
velled at the dulness of my understanding,
which should have prevented my perceiving it before; for every single circumstance
that had happened pointed but in one direction, and that was towards the end which
I had but just reached.

It was as plain as the light of day that
when Captain Leach went aboard of the
pirate craft on the night of the 21st of July,
Captain England would require him to ex-

plain his object in betraying the *Cassandra* into their hands; and it was equally plain that Leach would have to tell the truth; for it was not likely that he could deceive such a sharp and cunning blade as that famous freebooter. I recalled the strange look which Captain England had given me when he told me that Captain Leach had been "shot by accident" upon their coming aboard the *Cassandra;* whereupon, regarding matters from my present stand-point, I felt assured that England had killed Leach with his own hand, so that with him the secret of the stone might perish from amongst them. I also felt convinced that he must, with great care and circumspection, have picked the lock of the despatch-box and have despoiled it of its contents, which he had kept for himself without informing any of his shipmates of what he had found.

I could not at first account for the treatment that I had met with at the pirates' hands, nor why I had not been shot so soon as I had stepped upon their decks, for it was plain to see that that would be the easiest and quickest way for Captain England to rid himself of me; yet it was very apparent to me that he desired that my life should be saved, and was even inclined to show me some kindness after his own fashion; and I do verily believe that that wicked and bloody man entertained a sincere regard for my person, and had it in his mind to do me a good turn; for even the very worst of men have some seed of kindness in them, otherwise they could not be of our human brotherhood, but wild beasts, thinking only of rending and tearing one another.

But I could easily perceive that so soon as England felt assured of my coming aboard of his craft, he would strive to mislead me into thinking that he knew nothing of the stone, lest by some inadvertent word I should betray a knowledge of it to the others, and he would have to share his spoil with them. Therefore he would carefully lock the box again, and would toss it in the corner to lead me to think he knew nothing of the contents.

All this train of reasoning I followed out in my mind, and when I recalled the quizzical, cunning look which the rogue had given me when I asked for the despatch-box, I felt certainly assured that I was right.

I remember that when I had clearly cogitated all this out in my own mind I felt as though one step had been gained towards the recovery of the stone, and for an instant it seemed as though a great part of the weight of despondency had been lifted from my breast. But the next moment it settled upon me again when I brought to mind that I was as far as ever from regaining the jewel; for I knew not where the pirates then were, and even if I did know, and was venturesome enough to face their captain a second time, it was not likely that he would be so complacent as to give back such a great treasure for the mere asking.

Nor do I think it likely that I would ever have gained anything by this knowledge which had come to me (unless I might have used it to help my case with the East India Company) had not Providence seen fit to send me help in a most strange and unexpected manner. And thus it was:

One morning when I came upon deck I saw several of the passengers, together with the captain and the first mate, standing at the lee side of the ship and looking out forward, Captain Croker with a glass to his eye. Upon inquiring they told me that the lookout had some little time before sighted a small open boat, which had been signalling the ship with what they were now able to make out was a shirt tied to the blade of an oar. We ran down to the boat, which we reached in twenty or thirty minutes, and then hove to, and it came alongside.

There were three men in her, who seemed to be in a mightily good condition for castaways in an open boat.

I stood looking down into it along with other of the passengers, watching the men as they took in their oars and laid them along the thwarts. Just then one of the fellows raised his face and looked up; and when I saw him I could not forbear a sudden exclamation of amazement. I remember one of my fellow-passengers, a Mr. Wilson, who stood next to me, asked me what was the matter. I made some excuse or other that was of little consequence, but the truth was that I recognized the fellow as that very pirate who had first kicked me in the loins when I lay bound upon the deck of the *Cassandra*, and whom Captain England had knocked down with the iron belaying-pin.

However, the fellow did not recognize me, for I was a very different object now than when he had seen me lying upon the pirate deck, pinched with my sickness, barefoot and half naked, and my cheeks and chin covered over with a week's growth of beard.

The three fellows presently came aboard, and were brought aft to the quarter-deck, where Captain Croker stood, just below the rail of the deck above. They told a very straightforward story, and I could not help admiring at their coolness and the clever way in which they passed it off. They said that they had been part of the crew of the brigantine *Ormond*, which had been lost in a storm about a hundred and twenty leagues north of the island of Madagascar. That the captain and six of the crew had taken the long-boat, and that they had become separated from her in the darkness two nights before. They answered all of Captain Croker's questions in a very straightforward manner, and with all the appearance of truth. After satisfying himself, he told them that they might go below and get something to eat, and that he would carry them to England as a part of the ship's crew.

At first I was inclined to tell the real

THE THREE FELLOWS WERE BROUGHT AFT TO THE QUARTER-DECK, WHERE CAPTAIN CROKER STOOD, JUST BELOW THE RAIL OF THE DECK ABOVE.

truth concerning them to Captain Croker, but on second thoughts I determined to see what the fellows had to say for themselves; for I only recognized one of them, and, after all, their story might be true, and that one have given up his wicked trade in the four or five months since I had last seen him.

About an hour after this I saw my friend the pirate engaged forward in coiling a rope. I came to him and watched him for a while, but he kept steadily on with what he was about, and said nothing to me.

"Well, sir," said I, after a bit, "and how was Captain England when you saw him last?"

The fellow started up as suddenly as though the rope had changed to an adder in his hands. He looked about him as though to see if any one were near and had overheard what I said to him, and then recovered himself with amazing quickness. He grinned in a simple manner, and chucked his thumb up to his forelock. "What was it you were saying, sir?" says he. "I didn't just understand you."

"Come, come," said I; "that will never pass amongst old friends. Why, don't you remember me?"

He looked at me in a mightily puzzled fashion for a while. "No, sir; asking your pardon, sir," said he, "I don't remember you."

"What!" said I, "have you forgot Captain Mackra, and how you gave him a kick in the side when he lay on the deck of the *Cassandra*, down off Juanna?" As the fellow looked at me I saw him change from red to yellow and from yellow to blue; his jaw dropped, and his eyes started as though a spirit from the dead had risen up from the decks in front of him. "So," said I, "I see you remember me now."

"For God's sake, sir," said he, "don't ruin a poor devil who wants to make himself straight with the world. I was drunk when I kicked you, sir—the Lord knows I was;

you wouldn't hang me for that, sir, would you?"

"That depends," said I, sternly, "upon whether you answer my questions without telling me a lie, as you did Captain Croker just now."

"I wish I may die, sir," said he, "if what I tell you ain't so. We all three of us left the *Royal James* last night—she was the *Cassandra*, sir, but we christened her a new name, and hoisted the Black Roger over her. We got scared, sir, at the way things was going since Ned England left us and Tom Burke turned captain; for he ain't the man England was, and that's the truth. All we ask now, sir, is to start fair and square again; and so be if we don't hang for this, I wish I may be struck dead, sir, if I, for one, go back to the bloody trade again. So all I want is to have a fair trial, and I begs of you, sir, that you won't say the word that would hang us all up to the yard-arms as quick as a wink."

I am mightily afraid that I did not hear the last of the fellow's discourse, for one part of the speech that he had 'dropped went through me like a shot. "How is that?" I cried. "Was not Captain England with you when you deserted the ship?"

"Why, no, sir," says he. "You see, sir, when we sailed away from Juanna, Tom Burke began to move heaven and earth against England, and back of him he had all of the worst of the crew aboard. First of all he began setting matters by the ears because England and Ward had been wheedled into giving you — asking your pardon, sir — a good sound vessel and all them bales of cloth stuff. I tell you plain, sir, Burke would never have let you had 'em if he hadn't wanted to use the matter against England. Well, sir, one night Ward fell overboard—nobody knowed how—and there was an end of him. After that they weren't long in getting rid of England, I can tell you."

"Yes, yes," I cried, impatiently, "but how did you get rid of him?"

"Why, sir," says he, "they marooned him on a little island off the Mauritius, and six others with him; they was—"

"Never mind them," I cried; "but tell me, do you know what became of him?"

"Why, yes, sir," says he; "leastways we knew of him by hearsay; and this was how: About eight weeks ago we ran into a cove on the south shore of Mauritius to clean both ships, which had grown mightily foul. While we lay there on the careen a parcel of the crew who had been off hunting for game fetched back one of the self-same fellows we had marooned two months and more before. · He told us that England and his shipmates had made a little craft out of bits of boards and barrel-staves, and had crossed over to the Mauritius in a spell of fair weather, though it was five leagues and more away."

To all this I listened with the greatest

intentness. " And is that all you know of him?" said I. "And can you not tell wheth-er he is yet on the island ?"

The fellow looked at me for a moment out of the corners of his eyes without speaking. " Look 'ee, sir," said he, after a little while, "what I wants to know is this: be ye seeking to harm Ned England or not ?"

" And do you trouble yourself about that?" says I. " Sure he can be no friend of yours, for did I not myself see him knock out a parcel of your teeth with an iron be-laying-pin ?"

" Yes, you did," says he; " but I bear him no grudge for that."

" Why," said I, " then neither do I bear him a grudge, and I give you my word of honor that I mean no harm to him."

The fellow looked at me earnestly for a while. " You wants to know where Ned England is, don't you, sir?" said he.

I nodded my head.

"And I wants to be perserved from hanging, don't I?"

I nodded my head again.

"Then look 'ee, sir," says he, "we'll strike a bit of a bargain: if you'll promise to say nothing to harm me and my shipmates, I'll tell you where to find Ned England."

I considered the matter for a while. The fellow had told me a straightforward story, nor did I doubt that he intended to break away from his evil courses. I may truly say that I verily believe I would not have betrayed the three poor wretches under any circumstances. "Very well," said I, "I promise to keep my part of the bargain."

"Upon your honor?" said he.

"Upon my honor," said I.

"Then, sir," said he, "you will find him at Port Louis, in the Mauritius," and he turned upon his heel and walked away.

13

XV.

I WAS filled with the greatest exultation by the knowledge which I had gained through the deserter from the pirates, for not only had I discovered the whereabouts of the one man in all of the world whom I felt well convinced had knowledge of the Rose of Paradise, but that man no longer had a crew of wicked and bloody wretches back of him, but stood, like me, upon his own footing. Therefore I determined that I would by some means or other either regain the treasure or perish in the attempt, for I would rather die than live a life of dishonor such as now seemed to lie before me. However, I plainly perceived that if I would recover the treasure I would have to escape from the ship by some means or other whilst we were upon our passage and near the isle of Mauritius, for if I lost time by going home and standing my examination, many things might occur which would lose the chance to me forever: England might quit the Mauritius, or gather together another crew of pirates upon his own account, for with such a treasure as the Rose of Paradise he had it clearly in his power to do that and much more.

At that time our English vessels were used to lay their course up and down the Mozambique Channel, and not along the eastern coast of Madagascar; for the Mauritius and other islands which lie to the north-east of that land belong to the French or Dutch, as those in the Channel belong to us. Therefore it was necessary to my purpose that I should persuade Captain Croker to alter his course, so as to run down outside the island instead of through the Channel, for it was plain to see that even if I should be able to escape from the *Lavinia* to Juanna or to any of the coadjacent islands, I would be as far as ever from getting to Mauritius, which lieth many leagues away around the northern end of Madagascar.

So I determined to make a clean breast of it, and confide the whole plan to Captain Croker from beginning to end, only I would say nothing as to how I had gained my knowledge of England's whereabouts, for I would not break the promise which I had given to the deserter, as told above.

As no time was to be lost in following out the plans which I had determined upon, I requested that I might have speech with Captain Croker that very night. I told him everything concerning the affair from beginning to end, adding nothing and omitting nothing. Although so old and so well-tried a friend, he was cast into the utmost depths of wonder and amazement at my audacity in proposing that he should alter the course of his vessel, and at my boldness in daring to tell him my plans for escaping from the restraint under which I had been placed. He questioned me closely concerning many matters: as to what led me to think that England was the present possessor of the jewel; as to how I proposed to proceed after I had escaped to the land; and as to how I had become informed of the pirate's whereabouts, concerning which last particular I would give him no satisfaction.

I knew not what he had in his mind, nor where all these questions tended, and by-and-by left the cabin, though in a sad state of uncertainty, not knowing how Captain Croker inclined, nor what might be his feelings in regard to me.

Nor was my uncertainty lessened for several days, in which time I knew not what to think, but waited for some sign from him. One evening, however, the whole matter was resolved in a most simple, natural, and unexpected manner.

At that time we were about seventy or eighty leagues north of the island of Mada-

gascar. All the passengers being at supper, with Captain Croker at the head of the
table, conversation began to run upon those
pirates who had much infested these waters
of late.

"Why," says Captain Croker, "the presence of the rascals has so affected me that
I have determined to alter the course of my
vessel, and to run outside of Madagascar instead of through the Mozambique Channel,
for it is well to have plenty of sea-room
either to fight or to run from these wicked
rogues. So now, if the wind holds good,
seeing we are such friends with the French-
men in these peaceful days, I purpose stopping at the Mauritius to take aboard fresh
provisions."

Captain Croker did not look at me whilst
he was saying all this, but studiously kept
his eyes upon the plate before him, and
presently rose and left the table.

As for me, I sat with my heart beating
within my breast as though it would burst

asunder, for I saw that my fate was decided
at last, and that one of the greatest happen-
ings in all of my life was soon to come upon
me.

In two days, as Captain Croker had pre-
dicted, we dropped anchor in the harbor off
Port Louis at about three o'clock in the afternoon. I ate but little supper that night,
my mind being so engrossed upon that
which I had undertaken to do.

We lay about half a mile from the shore,
the water in the bay being very calm and
still. I had procured four large calabash
gourds, with which I had made shift to rig
up a very decent float or life-preserver, for I
had need of some such aid in my expedition,
not being a very expert swimmer.

In all this time I had said nothing to Captain Croker, nor he to me; but about seven
o'clock, it being at that time pretty dark, he
came to me where I stood by the rail of the
poop-deck.

" Jack," said he, in a low voice, " are you

still in the mind for carrying this thing
through ?"

" Yes, I am," I said.

" To-night ?" says he.

" To-night," says I.

" Then God bless you !" said he, and he
gave my hand a hearty grip.   Then he
turned upon his heel and went below, and
I knew that my time for acting had arrived.

I had not much fear of sharks, for I had
seen enough of those cowardly creatures to
know that they rarely or never attack a
swimmer or a moving man, but only a body
floating upon the water as though dead;
moreover, at night they are asleep or in deep
water, for they are not often seen upon the
surface after the darkness has fairly fallen.

After the captain left me I looked around
and saw that no one else was nigh upon the
deck.   I took my calabash gourds and entered the boat that hung from the davits
astern.   Taking a hint from Captain Leach,
I had secured a coil of line by which I

might lower myself into the water, for if I
had dropped with a splash I would have
been pretty sure to have been discovered.
Having removed my shoes and stockings,
which I wrapped in a piece of tarpaulin,
together with my tinder-box and flint and
steel, all of which I secured upon my head,
and having slipped the cords which bound
the calabashes under my arms, I slid down
the line into the water astern.

Having committed my life into the keeping of Providence, I struck out boldly for the
shore, being aided by a current which set
towards it, and directing my course by the
lights which glimmered faintly in the distance. So I reached the beach, and built a
fire, whereby I dried my clothes. Then, having put on my shoes and stockings, which
had been kept pretty dry by the tarpaulin,
I walked up the beach in the direction of
the scattered row of houses which, the moon
having now risen, stood out very plain at
about a quarter of a mile distant.

I found the town to consist of a great straggling collection of low one-story buildings, mostly made of woven palm-branches, smeared over with mud which had dried in the sun. At this time it could not have been much less than nine o'clock, and all was dark and silent. I went aimlessly here and there, not knowing whither to direct my steps, until at last I caught sight of a little twinkle of light, which I perceived came through a crack of an ill-hung shutter. I went around to the front of the hut, which seemed larger and better made than others I had seen. Above the door hung an ill-made sign, and the moon shining full upon it, I could plainly see a rude picture of a heart with a crown above it, and underneath, written in great sprawling letters,—

"LE CŒUR DU ROY."

—From this I knew that it was an ordinary, at which I was greatly rejoiced, and also what suited me very well was to find that it was French, for I had no mind to fall in with English people just then, and I knew enough of French to feel pretty easy with the lingo. So into the place I stepped, as bold as brass, and ordered a glass of grog and something to eat.

There were perhaps half a score of rough, ill-looking fellows gathered around a dirty table playing at cards by the light from a flame of a bit of rope's-end stuck in a calabash of grease. They laid down their cards when I came in, and stared at me in a very forbidding fashion. However, I paid no attention to them, but sat down at a table at some little distance, and by-and-by the landlord, a little pot-bellied, red-faced Frenchman, brought me a glass of hot rum and a dish of greasy stew seasoned with garlic. He would have entered into talk with me, but I soon gave him to understand that I had no appetite for conversation just at this time; so after having made a bargain for lodgings during the night, he withdrew to a bench in the farther corner of the room, where I presently saw him fall asleep.

If I had hoped to escape from meeting my own countrymen, I soon discovered that I was to be sadly disappointed, for before I had been in the place a quarter of an hour I found that at least half the fellows around the table were Englishmen. They were the most villanous, evil-looking set of men that I had beheld in a long time, and I could not but feel uneasy, for I had with me gold and silver money to the value of between ten and eleven guineas, and by their muttering together and looking in my direction now and then I knew that they were talking concerning me.

Presently one of the fellows got up from the table and came over to the place where I sat.

" Look 'ee, messmate," said he, seating himself upon the corner of the table beside me; "be ye English, French, Dutch, Portuguese, or what ?"

At first I was of a mind to deny being an Englishman, but on second thoughts I perceived that it would be useless to do so, there being the scum of so many peoples at that place that I could not hope to escape exposure.

" Why, shipmate," said I, " I'm an Englishman."

" Where do ye hail from ?" said he.

" Over yonder," said I, pointing in the direction of the *Lavinia*.

" Did ye come aboard of the craft that ran into the harbor to-day ?"

I nodded my head.

" Did ye come ashore without leave ?"

I nodded my head again.

The others had all laid down their cards and were looking at us by this time, and I knew not what would have been the upshot of the matter had not the door just then been flung open and a great rough fellow come stumping into the place.

" Well," he bawled, in a loud, hoarse voice,

"poor Ned is on his way to h—l hot-foot to-night. I just came by his stew-hole over yonder. Pah!"—here the fellow spat upon the floor—"he was screeching and howling and yelling as though the d—l was basting him already."

"Who's with him now?" says one of the fellows at the table.

"Who's with him?" says the other, in a mightily contemptuous tone. "Why, d'ye think that anybody would be such a —— —— fool as to stay with him now, with nothing to be got for it but the black tongue and a cursing?"

"But what I say is this," said an ill-looking one-eyed fellow: "he's not the man to serve his trade for all these here years and nothing to show for it. It's all very well to say that Jack Mackra shot the hoops off his luck; but you mark my words, he's got a cable out to windward somewhere, and he ain't goin' to run on the lee shore with an empty hold."

I was so amazed to hear my own name spoken that I knew not at first whether to believe that which mine ears had heard or whether they had heard aright. Then it was as though a sudden light flashed upon me. I needed not the next speech to tell me everything.

"Well," says one of the fellows, "even if so be as Ned England is going to smell brimstone before this time to-morrow, I for one see no reason to lose our game. Come along, Blake," he sang out to the fellow who had been speaking to me, and who rejoined the others upon being bidden.

I was in a great ferment of spirits at all this, for I perceived very clearly that England was mightily sick, and perhaps dying, with that dangerous fever known as the "black tongue," from which it is a rare thing for a man to recover with his life.

I observed that the fellow who had lately come into the ordinary did not join in the game along with the rest, but sat looking on. By-and-by I contrived to catch his eye as he glanced in my direction, whereupon I beckoned to him, and he came over to the table where I sat. Only a few words passed between us, and those in a very low tone.

" Is Ned England all alone ?" said I.

" Yes," said he.

" Will you show me where he is ?" said I.

He shot a quick look at me from under his brows. " How much will you give ?"

" A guinea " said I.

" I'll do it."

" When ?"

" To-morrow morning."

That was all that passed, and then he moved away and joined the others at the table.

The next morning I purchased a good large pistol from mine host, for I saw that with such companions as I was like to fall in with I would need some sort of weapon to protect myself. Having loaded it with a brace of slugs, I thrust it in my belt, and then stepped out of the door, where I found my acquaintance of the night before waiting for me.

"Are you ready?" said I.

"Yes," said he, "I am; but I must see the color of your money before I go a single step."

"It is yellow," said I, and held the guinea out in the palm of my hand.

When he saw it his eyes shone like coals and his fingers began to twitch. "Hand it over," says he, "and I'll take ye straight."

"No, no," said I; "avast there, shipmate. You get your money when I see Captain Edward England, and not before."

"So be it," says he. "Lay your course straight ahead yonder, and I'll follow after and tell you how to go."

I looked coolly into the fellow's face, and could not help grinning. "Why," says I, "to tell the truth, shipmate" (here I drew my pistol out of my belt and cocked it), "I have no appetite for a knife betwixt the ribs;

14

so you'll just march ahead, and if you try any of your tricks I'll put a brace of bullets through your head as sure as you're alive."

The fellow looked at me for a while in a puzzled sort of way; then he grinned, and swinging on his heel strode away, I following close behind him with the pistol ready cocked in my hand. We went onward in this way for about half a mile, until we came to a little hut that stood by itself beyond the rest of the town. My guide stopped short about fifty paces away from the hut. "There's where you'll find Ned England," said he, "and I'll go no farther for ten guineas, for I've no notion of catching the black tongue; and if you'll hearken to a bit of advice, shipmate, you'll give it a wide berth yourself."

I felt assured the fellow was telling me the truth, so I paid him his guinea, and then turned away and left him standing where he was, and as I stopped in front of the hut and looked back I saw that the man was yet standing in the very same spot, staring after me.

I may confess that I myself was somewhat overcome with fear of the dreadful disease, wherefore I stood for a moment before I knocked upon the door. But I presently rallied myself, calling to mind that this was the only means of recovering the Rose of Paradise, even if it was at the risk of my own life; therefore I knocked loudly on the door with the butt of my pistol.

My guide, who stood still in the same place, called out to me that there was no one to hear my knocking; so I pushed open the door and entered the hut.

For a while I saw nothing, for it was very dark within. But I heard a hoarse and chattering voice, scarce above a whisper, crying continually, " Hard a-lee !—hard a-lee !—hard a-lee !"

Presently mine eyes became accustomed to the gloom, and I might see the things around more clearly. There, in the corner of the room, lying upon a mat of filthy rags, his body almost a skeleton, his bloodshot eyes glaring out from under his matted hair, I beheld the famous pirate, Captain Edward England.

THERE, IN THE CORNER, I BEHELD THE FAMOUS PIRATE, CAPTAIN EDWARD ENGLAND.

XVI.

I MAY truly say that when I saw the doleful state of the poor wretch, and how he lay there without so much as a single soul to moisten his lips or to give him a draught of cold water, I forgot mine own troubles for the time being, and thought only of his pitiable condition.

I sometimes misdoubt whether I should have felt grieved for such a wicked and bloody man, who had for years done nothing but commit the most dreadful crimes, such as murther and piracy and the like, yet seeing him thus prostrated, lying helpless, and deserted by all his kind, I could not help my bowels being stirred by compassion; wherefore I thought neither of the danger from his fever, nor of the many grievous injuries which he had done, both to myself and to others, but only of relieving his present distresses.

My first consideration was to make him more clean, wherefore I fetched some water from a rivulet which I had noticed flow nigh to that place, and washed his hands and face, and so much of his body as seemed to me fitting. Then I gathered some fresh palm-leaves, and covered them over with a bit of sail which I found rolled up in the back part of the hut, and having thus made thereof a clean and comfortable bed, I carried the poor wretch thither and laid him upon it.

As I had eaten nothing that morning, I went back into the town and bought a lump of meat and some fresh fruit, and then back again to the hut. I noticed here and there some that stood and looked after me, though they said nothing to me, nor molested me in any manner. I afterwards found that my guide had so spread the news of my going to England's hut that many knew it, and accredited me with being a friend of the pirate's, and even a partaker in his wicked and nefarious deeds. Whether it was from this or from fear of contagion of the fever I know not, but certain it is I was never once molested so long as I was upon that island.

When I returned to the hut it seemed to me that the sick man had less fever than when I left him, which perhaps happened from the refreshment of the washing that I had given him, though it might have been that the crisis of his distemper had arrived, and that his complaint had now lessened in its intensity.

Some time after mid-day I was sitting beside the sick man, fanning both him and myself, for though the nights were cool at this season of the year, the middle of the day was both exceeding hot and sultry. He had ceased in his incessant and continuous muttering and talking, and was now lying quite silent, though breathing short and quick with the fever.

Suddenly he spoke. " Who are you?" said he, in a quick, sharp voice.

I thought at first he was still rambling in his mind, but when I looked at him I saw that his bloodshot eyes were fixed upon me. I placed my hand upon his brow, and though still very hot, I fancied that the skin was not so dry nor so hard as it had been.

" Who are you?" said he again in the same tone.

" There," said I, " lie still and rest. You have been mightily sick."

" Is it Jack Mackra?" said he.

" Yes," said I.

" And what do you do here?" said he.

" I am come to care for you just now," said I; " but now rest quietly, for I will not answer one single question more, and that I promise you."

He did not seek to speak again, but lay quite still, as though meditating; and presently, as I sat fanning him, I saw him close

his eyes, and after a while, by his deep and
regular breathing, knew that he was asleep,
and that his fever had turned.

As I remember all the circumstances concerning these things, I think that up to this
time I had given little if any thought concerning the treasure of which I had been in
quest; but now, seeing the sick man fairly
asleep, and in what seemed to me a fair
way to mend, my mind went instantly back
to it again, for I felt well assured that I
should find it or some signs of it about the
place where I then was.

It is not needful to recount all the manner in which I prosecuted my search for the
gem, for not only did I examine every scrap
of paper about the place in hopes of finding
some matter concerning it, but I sounded
the walls, and pierced wellnigh every inch
of the dirt floor with a sharpened stick of
wood, but found not one single sign of it
anywhere. I even searched in the pockets
of the breeches which the sick man wore,

and of his coat and waistcoat, which hung against the wall, but discovered nothing to reward my search—all that I found there being a book of needles and thread, a tailor's thimble, a great piece of tobacco, such as seafaring men always carry with them, a ball of yarn about half the bigness of an orange, and a hasp-knife.

I cannot tell the bitter disappointment that took possession of me when my search proved to be of so little avail; for I had felt so sure of finding the jewel or some traces of it, and had felt so sure of being able to secure it again, that I could not bear to give up my search, but continued it after every hope had expired.

When I was at last compelled to acknowledge to myself that I had failed, I fell into a most unreasonable rage at the poor, helpless, fever-stricken wretch, though I had but just now been doing all that lay in my power to aid him and to help him in his trouble and his sickness. " Why should I not leave him to rot where he is?" I cried, in my anger; "why should I continue to succor one who has done so much to injure me, and to rob me of all usefulness and honor in this world?" I ran out of the cabin, and up and down, as one distracted, hardly knowing whither I went. But by-and-by it was shown me what was right with more clearness, and that I should not desert the poor and helpless wretch in his hour of need: wherefore I went back to the hut and fell to work making a broth for him against he should awake, for I saw that the fever was broken, and that he was like to get well.

I did not give over my search for the stone in one day, nor two, nor three, but continued it whenever the opportunity offered and the pirate was asleep, but with as little success as at first, though I hunted everywhere. As for Captain England himself, he began to mend from the very day upon which I came, for he awoke from his first sleep with his fever nigh gone, and all the madness cleared away from his head; but he never once, for a long while, spoke of the strangeness of my caring for him in his sickness, nor how I came to be there, nor of my reasons for coming. Nevertheless, from where he lay he followed me with his eyes in all my motions whenever I was moving about the hut.

One day, however, after I had been there a little over a week, against which time he was able to lie in a rude hammock, which I had slung up in front of the door, he asked me of a sudden if any of his cronies had lent a hand at nursing him when he was sick, and I told him no.

"And how came you to undertake it?" says he.

"Why," said I, "I was here on business, and found you lying nigh dead in this place."

He looked at me for a little while in a mightily strange way, and then suddenly burst into a great loud laugh. After that he lay still for a while, watching me, but presently he spoke again.

"And did you find it?" says he.

"Find what?" I asked, after a bit, for I was struck all aback by the question, and could not at first find one word to say. But he only burst out laughing again. "Why," says he, "you psalm-singing, Bible-reading, straitlaced Puritan skippers are as keen as a sail-needle; you'll come prying about in a man's house looking for what you would like to find, and all under pretence of doing an act of humanity, but after all you find an honest devil of a pirate is a match for you."

I made no answer to this, but my heart sank within me; for I perceived, what I might have known before, that he had observed the object of my coming thither.

He soon became strong enough to move about the place a little, and from that time I noticed a great change in him, and that he seemed to regard me in a very evil way. One evening when I came into the hut, after an absence in the town, I saw that he had taken down one of his pistols from the wall, and was loading it and picking the flint. He kept that pistol by him for a couple of days, and was forever fingering it, cocking it, and then lowering the hammer again.

I do not know why he did not shoot me through the brains at this time; for I verily believe that he had it upon his mind to do so, and that more than once. And now, in looking back upon the business, it appears to me to be little less than a miracle that I came forth from this adventure with my life. Yet had I certainly known that death was waiting upon me, I doubt that I should have left that place; for in truth, now that I had escaped from the *Lavinia*, as above narrated, I had nowhere else to go, nor could I ever show my face in England or amongst my own people again.

Thus matters stood until one morning the whole business came to an end so suddenly and so unexpectedly that for a long while I felt as though all might be a dream, from which I should soon awake.

We were sitting together silently, he in a very moody and bitter humor. He had his pistol lying across his knees, as he used to do at that time.

Suddenly he turned to me as though in a fit of rage. "Why do you stay about this accursed fever hole?" cried he; "what do you want here, with your saintly face and your godly airs?"

"I stay here," said I, bitterly, "because I have nowhere else to go."

"And what do you want?" said he.

"That you know," said I, "as well as I myself."

"And do you think," said he, "that I will give it to you?"

"No," said I, "that I do not."

"Look 'ee, Jack Mackra," said he, very

slowly, "you are the only man hereabouts who knows anything of that red pebble" (here he raised his pistol and aimed it directly at my bosom); "why shouldn't I shoot you down like a dog, and be done with you forever? I've shot many a better man than you for less than this."

I felt every nerve thrill as I beheld the pistol set against my breast, and his cruel, wicked eyes behind the barrel; but I steeled myself to stand steadily and to face it.

"You may shoot if you choose, Edward England," said I, "for I have nothing more to live for. I have lost my honor and all except my life through you, and you might as well take that as the rest."

He withdrew the pistol, and sat regarding me for a while with a most baleful look, and for a time I do believe that my life hung in the balance with the weight of a feather to move it either way. Suddenly he thrust his hand into his bosom and drew forth the ball of yarn which I had observed amongst other things in his pocket. He flung it at me with all his might, with a great cry as though of rage and of anguish. " Take it," he roared, " and may the devil go with you! And now away from here, and be quick about it, or I will put a bullet through your head even yet."

I knew as quick as lightning what it was that was wrapped in the ball of yarn, and leaping forward I snatched it up and ran as fast as I was able away from that place. I heard another roar, and at the same time the shot of a pistol and the whiz of a bullet, and my hat went spinning off before me as though twitched from off my head. I did not tarry to pick it up, but ran on without stopping: but even yet, to this day, I cannot tell whether Edward England missed me through purpose or through the trembling of weakness; for he was a dead-shot, and I myself once saw him snap the stem of a wineglass with a pistol bullet at an ordinary in Jamaica.

15

As for me, the whole thing had happened so quickly and so unexpectedly that I had no time either for joy or exultation, but continued to run on bareheaded as though bereft of my wits; for I knew I held in my hand not only the great ruby, but also my honor and all that was dear to me in my life.

But although England had so freely given me the stone, I knew that I must remain in that place no longer. I still had between five and six guineas left of the money which I had brought ashore with me when I left the *Lavinia*. With this I hired a French fisherman to transport me to Madagascar, where I hoped to be able to work my passage either to Europe or back to the East Indies.

As fortune would have it, we fell in with an English bark, the *Kensington*, bound for Calcut, off the north coast of that land, and I secured a berth aboard of her, shipping as an ordinary seaman; for I had no mind to tell my name, and so be forced to disclose the secret of the great treasure which I had with me. After arriving at Calcut I was fortunate enough to be able to find a vessel ready to sail for Bombay, whereon I secured a berth, and so arrived safe at that place about the middle of March.

I had unrolled the ball of yarn and looked at the stone so soon as I had been able to do so after getting it into my possession. Then, finding that it was safe and unhurt, as I had seen it last, I had rolled it up again, for I could perceive that there was no better hiding-place for it than the one the cunning pirate had provided. So for all this last voyage I had carried a fortune of three hundred and fifty thousand pounds in my pocket, wrapped up in a ball of yarn.

It was early in the morning when we arrived at Bombay, and so soon as I was able I disclosed my name and condition to the captain under whom I had sailed, and con-

trived to impress him with the importance
of my commission, without disclosing anything to him in regard to the stone. He
was very complacent to me, and would have
had me dress myself in a more fitting manner, and in some of his own clothes, for I
was clad no better than the other seamen
with whom I had consociated for all this
time; but I was too impatient to delay my
going ashore for one moment longer than
was needful, so he kindly sent me off without any further stay.

I went straight to the Residency, and
though the attendants would have stayed
me, I so insisted, both with words and with
force, that they were constrained to show
me directly into the presence of the Governor.

I found him seated with Mistress Pamela
at breakfast, beneath the shade of a wide
veranda overlooking a beautiful and luxuriant garden. The Governor arose as I came
forward, looking very much surprised at my

boldness in so forcing my presence upon his privacy. As for Mistress Pamela, I beheld her eyes grow wide and her face as white as marble, and thereby knew that she had recognized me upon the instant.

I came direct to the table, and drawing forth the jewel, still wrapped in the yarn (for my agitation had been so great that I had not thought to unroll the covering from the stone), I laid it upon the table, with my hands trembling as though with an ague.

"What does all this mean?" cried the Governor. "Who are you, and what do you want?" For I was mightily changed in my appearance by the rough life through which I had passed, and he did not recognize me.

But I only pointed to the ball of yarn. "Open it," I cried; "for God's sake, open it!"

I saw a sudden light come into Mistress Pamela's eyes. She clasped her hands, and repeated after me, "Open it, open it!"

The Governor himself seemed to be impressed by our emotion; for, instead of troubling himself to unwind the yarn, he snatched up a bread-knife and cut through the strands, so that they fell apart, and the jewel rolled out upon the white linen table-cover.

The Governor gazed upon it as though thunderstruck. Presently he slowly raised his eyes and looked at me. "What is this?" said he.

In the mean time I had somewhat recovered from my excessive emotion. "Sir," said I, "it is the Rose of Paradise."

"And you?"

"I am Captain John Mackra."

The Governor grasped my hand, and shook it most warmly. "Sir," said he, "Captain Mackra, I am vastly delighted to find you such a man as my niece has always maintained you to be. The little rebel has led me a most disturbed and disquieted life ever since I was constrained to order you back to England under restraint. I now leave you a captive in her hands, trusting to her to give you a famous dish of tea, whilst I go and consign this great treasure to some place of safe-keeping. I shall soon return, for I am most impatient to hear your narrative of those events which led to the recovery of this stone."

So saying, he turned and left us, bearing the Rose of Paradise with him, and I sat down to a dish of tea with Mistress Pamela.

When the Governor returned he had first to listen to other matters than those concerning the Rose of Paradise; for, with his consent, Pamela Boon had promised to be my wife.

THE END.